ANGELIC HOSTS

Angelic Hosts: Discovering Hosts of the Heavenly Kind

Copyright © 2019 Brian Guerin

ISBN: 9781076134196

*Cover design, typeset, & development by Tall Pine Books.

|| Printed in the United States of America

ANGELIC HOSTS

DISCOVERING HOSTS OF THE HEAVENLY KIND

BRIAN GUERIN

BridalGlory.com

CONTENTS

INTRODUCTION

The letter alone kills but the Spirit gives life. I've always been one who can't merely read the Word, I've got to experience the Word. What is Christianity if not *experiential*? My aim with this book is simple: to raise expectations for encounters, namely *angelic activity* in your own life. This biblically dominant force is often overlooked in our day to day routines. I pray that by and through these chapters, you will find yourself growing with expectation to partner with God's angelic realm.

Prior to producing this material, I had a dream in which a doctor approached a person who was struggling with their eyesight. I sensed that the doctor represented the angelic. In this dream the patient didn't actually realize that they had a problem with their eyes, yet the doctor approached, inspected, and assisted in opening the patient's eyes to be able to see clearly. I knew that this represented angelic aid in opening spiritual eyes.

Like in the dream, we often aren't able to recognize our own blindness. We don't recognize *blind spots* because they are just that...blind spots. We don't have the capacity to measure our visual capability in the spirit. We must have our eyes opened to be able to see the unseen with 20/20 vision. Dreams, visions, and trances are ever available, yet an opening of the eyes is required. I pray that through this book, you'll step into a 20/20 awakening, as it were—that you would *see* and *know* that which is occurring in the spirit realm around you. May angelic aid be available to aid, assist and encounter you as you step forward in your journey!

1

NECESSITY AND EXPECTANCY

KNOWING YOUR ANGELIC NEEDS

ANGELS ARE MENTIONED OVER 270 TIMES IN SCRIPTURE. FAR too often, we are influenced by a religious spirit, quite frankly, and we are talked out of our inheritance which includes partnership with the angelic. This is not the time nor the season to be walking in 30% or 40% of God's kingdom. It is time that we walk in 100% of the kingdom of God and His angelic resources. It is time to fire on all cylinders. We see darkness covering the earth in these days, as the Bible speaks of, but at the same time—we see the glory of God covering the world as well. When the world makes a move, God is already several steps ahead. It is the blessed benefit of serving an omniscient Creator! Jesus said, "Greater works you will do..." (see John 14:12)

Some rebut with, "Yeah, but He was only talking about quantity because He was only doing ministry for three years." No, it is both quantity and quality. Why? Because it is Him doing it to begin with! When Christ promised us greater works, He wasn't removing Himself from the equation. He was essentially saying, "I'll be doing greater works through you." Jesus' garment was touched and a woman was healed. Decades later, Paul had sweaty work rags taken from him and placed on the demon possessed and they were healed. Do you see the upgrade? Greater works were already beginning in the record of Acts and greater works are still continuing to this day. Besides, whether it was a pinky being healed or someone walking out of a wheelchair, it's all Jesus anyway.

A religious spirit will attempt to talk you out of these things. A religious spirit will convince you that you'll be easily deceived when you begin tapping into miracles, healings and the angelic realm. Yet, the Bible is littered with authentic angelic encounters, sent from God, and God wasn't in paranoia regarding His people and their relationship to angels.

Anytime that I've encountered angels in my life, I've never been drawn to worship them or found myself distracted from Christ. In fact, God-sent angels always pull you toward Jesus. They don't want the attention. Folks often mean well when they attempt to warn us of deception. Yet despite being well meaning, many people are hindering others from stepping into the fulness of what God has. Someone might begin to speak about sensing an angel in their midst and a well meaning brother says, "Well, you better be careful of deception...even the elect can be deceived." Then suddenly that person withdraws from their experience, shuts down sensitivity to angels and lives in a fear of deception. This isn't God's best.

The Lord Jesus is inexhaustible. His Kingdom, His realms, His glory, graces, resources, angel armies, clouds of witnesses, signs and wonders, and so forth are absolutely inexhaustible. To box God into a theological framework that doesn't match up with Scripture is to limit our potential in experiencing and walking in the fullness of the Kingdom.

Much of the religious thinking regarding angels stems from a fear of deception. The problem is, that which you fear you ultimately become subject to. If you fear it, you will eventually be mastered by it. Therefore, when you are fearful and intimidated by the thought of deception, it is very, very easy to step into deception itself. Many spouting, "Don't be deceived," are actually deceived themselves while walking in 1% of the Kingdom when they're called to 100% of the Kingdom. Satan loves to limit access to these things by twisting pet Scriptures to hinder our vision.

Some of you reading this might have limited-to-no experience of angels in your life. Others might have seen sporadic glimpses of angels at work in your midst. Regardless of where you are with it, God wants to release constant availability to you in this realm. It's what we see in Scripture and it's what is intended for our lives. As we grow and learn in these areas, we experience enlightenment and understanding. As our enlightenment and understanding grows, we increase in faith and expectancy and the encounters only increase as a result. Thus we find ourselves in a divine cycle of visitation and habitation concerning angels.

ANGELIC ATTRIBUTES

"Are they (angels) not all ministering spirits sent out to serve for the sake of those who are to inherit salvation?" (Hebrews 1:14 emphasis added)

We can spot from the text that angels are spirits. While they might manifest looking like people at times, they are not people. They come from an eternal realm and exist outside of time. From this passage we also see that they are ministers. They are servants. They love to do the will of God. Not only that, but they have a specific focus on ministry to those who will inherit salvation and those who have inherited salvation. To those not walking in the Kingdom, angelic activity can be minimal or even nonexistent.

Sometimes in life, we find ourselves experiencing duplicity and multiplicity in our interests, affections and paths. Perhaps for a season you find yourself straying from the sole focus of your calling or dabbling in other things that God hasn't ordained. Unlike us, angels are singularly focused in their purpose and intent. The angels assigned to you have one job: assist you in your calling. They are continually assisting, serving and ministering to you with the ultimate goal of enabling you to walk out the fullness of your destiny. The blueprint we see in Scripture is the angelic encountering great generals like Jacob, Paul, Peter, Mary, Daniel, Moses, Joshua, Gideon and others. Again, if these men and women who went about great exploits for God and had need of an angelic visitation, how much more could we use them today? In fact the Word describes Christ encountering angels in this way:

> "Jesus said to him, 'Again it is written, 'You shall not put the Lord your God to the test." Again, the devil took him to a very high mountain and showed him all the kingdoms of the world and their glory. And He said to him, 'All these I will give you, if you will fall down and worship me.' Then Jesus said to him, 'Be gone, Satan! For it is written, 'You shall worship the Lord your God and Him only shall you serve.' Then the devil left him, and behold, angels came and were ministering to him.'" (Matthew 4:7-11)

If the perfect, spotless Son of God in the flesh needed angelic support, how much more do we need it as well? He is the highest standard. He is the perfect model of what life in a physical body should look like here on earth. Don't miss these quick passages on angelic help. You can't afford to miss out on the assistance that Christ Himself needed in the earth.

> "Yet You have made him a little lower than the heavenly beings and crowned him with glory and honor. You have given him dominion over the works of your hands; You have put all things under his feet." (Psalm 8:5-6)

The phrase heavenly beings in this passage, of course, refers to angels. This passage reveals that there is a ranking and an order among created beings. As of now, we sit slightly below angels in our rank. A New Testament passage reflects this same passage:

> "What is man, that you are mindful of him, or the son of man, that you care for him? You made him for a little while lower than the angels; you have crowned him with glory and honor, putting everything in subjection under his feet." (Hebrews 2:6-8)

Notice, angels are superior currently. Some speculate that there will be a day when that shifts as the Scripture says, "Beloved, we are God's children now, and what we will be has not yet appeared; but we know that when He appears we shall be like Him, because we shall see Him as He is" (1 John 3:2 emphasis added). Also, Paul points out, "Do you not know that we are to judge angels?" (1 Corinthians 6:3)

Why does this matter? Because for the time being, we find ourselves in a lower rank than angels, as a result, their activity isn't to be overlooked, neglected or scoffed at. There is a natural honor that flows upward when we understand these things. Whether it was Peter being freed from jail by an angel or an angel speaking out of the burning bush—biblical figures needed this presence and so do we. Angels carry the voice of the Lord and provide commissionings and sendings. They sometimes communicate in parables and sometimes provide insight and revelation. Essentially, an angel is like a microphone in the hand of God, amplifying the Lord's voice to you personally in a variety of ways. As this book unfolds, we'll target several of these functions. These realities and characteristics ought to stir faith and expectancy within you. They should highlight and exemplify our need for more.

> "Jacob left Beersheba and went towards Haran. And he came to a certain place and stayed there that night, because the sun had set. Taking one of the stones of the place, he put it under his head and lay down in that place to sleep." (Genesis 28:10-11)

Notice, Jacob came to a certain place, the Bible says. God loves places. He loves specific spots and regions to be markers for glory. As you journey with Jesus you'll find that particular regions, places, perhaps spots in your home and so forth become portals, openings and gateways for heaven and the angelic. Let's continue:

> "And he dreamed, and behold, there was a ladder set up on the earth, and the top of it reached to heaven. And behold, the angels of God were ascending and descending on it!" (Genesis 28:12)

This is absolutely a flagship set of Scriptures on the subject of angels. The angels in this passage first ascended up to heaven. After that, what did they do? They descended to the earth! Notice the motion and path of travel for angels. They relocate back and forth between the presence of God and the earth. Angels are not omnipresent. They cannot be everywhere at once, like God can. However, because they exist in the spirit-world, they are able to transport anywhere in the earth in the blink of an eye. They are limited to one space in time but they aren't limited in their ability to get there quickly. Humans are bound by natural laws of physics and gravity. Angels are not subject to such things. Many people think that angels merely exist in the heavens. However, as we've seen—they are quite busy in the earth and in their ministry. The passage goes on to say:

> "And behold, the Lord stood above it and said, 'I am the Lord, the God of Abraham your father and the God of Isaac. The land on which you lie I will give to you and to your offspring. Your offspring shall be like the dust of the earth, and you shall spread abroad to the west and to the east and to the north and to the south, and in you and your offspring shall all the families of the earth be blessed. Behold, I am with you and will keep you wherever you go, and will bring you back to this land. For I will not leave you until I have done what I have promised you.'" (Genesis 28:13-15)

What we see in this declaration is the Lord gives a blessing, a commissioning, and a promise given. All of them are tied into angelic encounters. Many either see the ladder alone with angels or see the blessing which God gave afterward. However, they are both linked. God is at the top of the ladder providing the commissioning, promise and blessing. We are on the receiving end at the bottom of the ladder. And angels are running up and down on the ladder communicating and assisting in fulfilling the commissions and promises God gave to us.

We are much more fluid, effective and useful in the earth when we align ourselves to these realities. It isn't complicated. In fact, it is the opposite of complicated. Angelic help makes things easier. You might say, "Where does the Holy Spirit work in all of this?" He is the general of the angelic realm in the earth! It is the protocol of heaven. I love it all, because it's all from Jesus! These things are found in Him and working through Him.

Angels are a means to an end. They are not an end in themselves. I like to use this example: imagine that God is a Gardener who commissions you to help Him plant and cultivate a piece of ground. He has a garden with soil, seeds, water, and sunshine to assist in the process. In order to grow plants, you need to watch the weather, plant at the appropriate time, till the soil, work the ground, use a watering can, and monitor the growth. It would be odd to simply focus on the Gardener and consider the till, the rake, and the watering can distractions, wouldn't it? Yet so many people do this with the angelic realm.

The angelic is a mere tool used to get the job done. Yet so many are ignoring the tools and just expecting the Gardner to do it all. Allow God to open up your awareness of His tool kit in your life. Embrace your need for this realm and consider the necessity of angels in your present circumstances. In this, you'll posture yourself properly and you will become an attractant to these heavenly beings.

2

ANGELIC RECORDS

MY PERSONAL HISTORY WITH ANGELS

THE FOURTH WATCH IN PRAYER IS VERY SIGNIFICANT TO ME. IF you don't know what that is, it's the hours between 3 a.m. and 6 a.m. It's actually when Jesus walked on water in the Scriptures. I had an encounter in this fourth watch which took place somewhere around 2007 or 2008 and has continued since. I was asleep and my laptop was sitting next to my bed on the nightstand, where it usually stays. It was unplugged. Nobody touched it. The power was off and yet the laptop supernaturally turned on. I felt a presence in the room—an angelic presence.

Many people feel God in the room and they just automatically say that it was the Holy Spirit, yet often it could be that an angel just stepped next to you. You'll feel God because they come directly from the presence of the Lord. Their presence can cause electronics to do weird things and for stuff to shift in the room. I was enthralled by this sign and wonder from the Lord. I had been waking up to pray every morning at 3 a.m., so to have this supernatural turn-on was a wonder to me to meet heaven in that hour.

So, this encounter continued to happen and I even got it on video. I'd wake up a few minutes before 3 a.m. and film this thing turning on. I was hungry for God and wanted to know beyond a doubt if this was Jesus Christ Himself walking into my room, an angel or something else. So during this season of pressing in, I was asleep and woke up one night to the sound of rustling in my bedroom. I looked over by the dresser and saw about a foot long beam of light shoot across my room, hit my laptop and turn it on. It was 12:28 a.m. I knew it was representative of Genesis 12:28, which we read in the last chapter. It was a confirmation to me that this was a heavenly invasion of the angelic realm that was causing my laptop to turn on.

When these encounters would happen, revelation would flow. I couldn't journal fast enough! I'd see visions, pictures and downloads. It was an awakening to me in the angelic realm. I was hungry and God provided experiential encounter with wonders and confirmation. You see, hunger is of paramount importance. While God is certainly sovereign and dominant, you have to understand the kingdom of heaven is also very gentle and sensitive. It's sort of like water. It will flow to the places with least resistance. When there is little resistance to the Kingdom, the Kingdom will flow like Niagara Falls.

What is resistance? It's things like unbelief, wrong beliefs, bad teaching, false perceptions, lack of understanding and so forth. Once you eliminate these barriers of resistance, the Kingdom breaks in. When the Kingdom begins to flow in your life, it's a deluge that isn't easy to stop.

The angelic realm is the same way. You might be closed off to the experience of angels as a believer. Despite this resistance, they'll still work on your behalf and give assistance for you are a child of God. Yet you won't pick up on the activity and you certainly won't see the sensational break-in of angels like God desires for you.

THE OPENING OF THE FAUCET

The angelic realm is a massive facet of Kingdom function. For me personally, I sort of stumbled into the angelic. I didn't intentionally set out to explore it. I was simply loving Jesus—which is always the gateway. No one gets to the experience of the Father by bypassing King Jesus Himself. So I was loving Jesus and locked away in the closet for awhile. It was prior to going into ministry or anything else. In fact, it was prior to the angelic-laptop encounter I shared previously.

As I was praying in my room, the doorknob to my door began to turn. I checked the door. I knew no one was in the house. I quickly looked at the time and it was 5:39 a.m. The Lord spoke to me that from May 3rd until the 9th, I was to be locked away in prayer and God would open up the door and come in. May 3rd came around. I sought God all day. Nothing happened. May 4th came, nothing happened. Then the 5th, 6th, 7th, and 8th came—I sought God all day and yet, nothing happened. The Lord will sometimes bring us into extended days of seeking in order to take us deeper in Him. Deep things belong to those who will go deep. Staying shallow won't get you there.

May 9th came around, and I was a bit discouraged to be honest with you. I was up early seeking God and then went to take a power nap so that I could jump back into prayer afterward. As soon as my head hit my pillow (like Jacob's head on the rock), the doorknob to the bedroom turned. From there, the door actually opened and I could see a ladder. It was Jacob's ladder. It was a gorgeous, blinding white ladder that went up into the heavens. I couldn't tell if it was an open vision or a physical reality.

You have to understand, I wasn't seeking this. I wasn't really going after the angelic realm. I was just going after the Lord. It was God's idea to break this facet into my walk. From this encounter with Jacob's angelic ladder, run-ins with angels became constant in my life. You can ask my kids; angels manifest in our midst frequently now. It might sound out there to some, but my kids and I could just be talking about the Lord and we can hear angels walking in the room.

This moment during a lockup in May released a deluge of supernatural moments with angels that continue to this day. Some might think, why would Jesus use angels like this? Doesn't that distract people from Himself? Absolutely not! Jesus is not insecure about His position. He wants us to be on board with all of His features and facets.

Some say, "Yeah but Jacob's ladder was Old Testament, not New." Firstly, Old Testament does not necessarily mean antiquated and irrelevant. Beyond that, Jesus referenced this also by saying, "Truly, truly, I say to you, you will see heaven opened, and the angels of God ascending and descending on the Son of Man" (John 1:51). These are things to believe for and to stretch for with expectancy. Often, if I feel that heaven wants me to emphasize the angelic in a meeting, I'll pray this verse over the congregation.

I was in Arizona ministering and the Lord had me bring emphasis to this topic. I preached on it and generally at the end of a session like this I will pray for the alignment of God's people with God's Kingdom in every way. If Jesus said that angels would ascend and descend on the Son of Man, then we can absolutely expect the angelic because the Son of Man resides in us! So we released these truths in this meeting and as I prayed this verse from John 15, one of the leaders on staff had a wonder manifest from the meeting. She had feathers upon feathers on her head. It was a wonder pointing to angelic presence.

Often, lights, gold dust, feathers, and gems are signs and wonders pointing to angels presence. In fact, angels often will deliver these things. The Bible describes manna being as angel food in Psalm 78. How do you think the manna was delivered to the Israelites? It wasn't merely brushed out of heaven onto the earth. It was delivered by the hands of angels.

Likewise, signs and wonders are often delivered in our midst by angels themselves. Light, heat, wind, and increased revelation all point to an angelic presence. Sometimes a new sense of authority if it's more of a warring angel drawing near. When we look at the Scriptures, we see that every generation needed angels manifesting. Who do we think we are to exempt ourselves? Consider the possibilities of an angel-less Bible:

- Peter would have never been freed from jail
- Paul wouldn't have had direction during the shipwreck on Malta
- The Son of God's birth wouldn't have been orchestrated and communicated like it was
- Moses never would have been commissioned at the burning bush
- Daniel wouldn't have had the revelation he had

We cannot afford to miss this. I was in Virginia preaching at the Virginia Tech campus. After the meetings we were in the campus cafeteria eating. It wasn't a spiritual setting by any means. As we were eating, a feather manifested out of thin air. It was a long, white feather. As it floated down, I caught it and immediately checked the time. Remember to check the time when you experience a manifestation. God can speak through such things. Sure enough, it was 1:51 p.m. and I immediately remembered John 1:51, regarding angels which we read earlier.

I was once preaching in Orlando and a couple of feathers started breaking into the meeting. I didn't know it at the time, but someone was FaceTiming with a girl who was in an entirely different city. We began pressing in for more and suddenly feathers manifested in a different city with the girl who was on the other end of the FaceTime.

I was preaching a meeting once and a gentleman kept seeing the silhouette of a man standing next to him. Every time he went to look, it was gone. He just saw the man sitting across the aisle from him. This happened repetitively throughout the meeting. What no one knew was that this man spent the last dollar he had to get to the meeting and had no money to get home. After the service, a man across the aisle came over, shook his hand, and gave him $500. The angel standing by him had caused this to happen. Remember, they have a job to minister and serve those who will inherit salvation.

We've seen manifestations that look like light orbs, pockets of energy, and more. I want these experiences to raise your faith and openness. These events are not random. Heaven does nothing by happenstance. The kingdom of darkness offers squirrely knock-off versions of these things that cause fear and deception, yet the kingdom of heaven offers authentic encounters that leave a glorious mark on our lives.

PERSONAL ANGELS

EXCLUSIVE CELESTIAL HELP

I ONCE HAD A VISION THAT INVOLVED ANGELIC ASSISTANCE. I was waiting on the Lord one morning and slipped into a vision in which I saw with crystal clarity a person run their car into mine from the front right while I was driving. Now, I know at times the devil will attempt to produce fear through scare tactics and dark thoughts. However, I knew that this was from the Lord. God was showing a plot planned against me. A messenger angel allowed me to see something coming against my life. As a result, I knew to pray against these things and partner with the will of God in prayer.

About a week later, I was driving my daughter to school and sure enough, a lady started coming toward us on the front right side. She absolutely was about to hit us. The breaks locked up, I turned the wheel, and we didn't hit. It would have been a very, very hard hit too. However, through the angelic I foresaw what was to come and the Lord protected us. By simply following the Lord, He will show you things to come and direct your prayers accordingly. People will look at your life and wonder how you were able to escape tragedy or miss out on the stuff that hit everybody else, and you will simply respond, "It's the favor of the Lord!"

In the brief story I just shared, you see the role of both revelation angels and protective angels. There are diversities of angels that all fulfill their function in God's arsenal. In Scripture we see worshipping angels, judgment angels, and even healing angels. We'll be getting into several of these kinds of angels throughout the book. Yet I want the focus of this particular chapter to be on the subject of personal angels.

"Bless the Lord, O you his angels, you mighty ones who do His word, obeying the voice of his word!" (Psalm 103:20)

Another translation says:

"Praise the Lord, you angels, you mighty ones who carry out His plans, listening for each of his commands." (Psalm 103:20 NLT)

IDENTIFYING YOUR ANGELS

The Scriptures say famously, "For He will command His angels concerning you to guard you in all your ways" (Psalm 91:11). We each have angels assigned to our lives to guard us in all of our ways. I would encourage you, learn about your angels. Ask the Lord to allow you to see them. Ask God what the name of your angels are. Generally, the name of your angels is very indicative of you and your calling.

I have seen my angels before. One of them, glorified, stands about nine feet tall and weighs approximately 400 pounds. When I've seen him in human form he was much less intimidating. He was kind, loving, and would give you the shirt off his back. I also know the name of my angel which is quite revelatory in nature.

Now, let me preface these things with this: seek understanding concerning these things for the right reasons. If your aim is to get squirrely and off into left field, God won't provide revelation concerning these matters because your heart is not in the right place. We don't seek to know these things for the sake of the encounter itself or so that we can act more spiritual than others. We seek enlightenment in these areas so that we can seek Jesus more closely. When you chase God, His purposes, and His will—He will provide these insights to better equip you in your destiny. For me, if I see it in Scripture, I say Lord, I've got to have it. I won't get off of this Scripture until I have it.

Notice, the Scripture we read earlier says that the angels will guard us in all our ways. Not just some of them. The angels attached to you have a sole focus. You are not their part time gig. Their full time endeavor is guiding, ministering, and serving your role and calling. However, we will not realize the full benefit of this angelic banquet until we step out and act. Think of it, if you show up to help a person move a couch—you cannot begin helping them until they get up and do their part. Likewise, the activation of the angelic requires your activation as well. There are contingencies in this thing. Look at this passage from Psalms:

"The angel of the Lord encamps around those who fear him, and delivers them." (Psalm 34:7)

Did you catch it? The passage says that the angel encamps around those who fear God. What is the promise? Angelic encampment and deliverance. What is the contingency? Fearing God. Many have a false idea of the angelic and believe that angels simply come and go as needed. As if angels are scurrying in and out of your life in a fickle manner. However, angels are actually on assignment.

"And calling to him a child, he put him in the midst of them and said, "Truly, I say to you, unless you turn and become like children, you will never enter the kingdom of heaven. Whoever humbles himself like this child is the greatest in the kingdom of heaven." (Matthew 18:2-4)

So Jesus begins teaching and calls a child to come to Him. From verse 4 onward, He continues to teach on the Kingdom. As we arrive to verse 10, Jesus utters a powerful truth with the child still on his lap:

"See that you do not despise one of these little ones. For I tell you that in heaven their angels always see the face of my Father who is in heaven." (Matthew 18:10)

The word their connotes ownership, in the verse we just read. It's not that the child owns the angel. However, their is a genuine reality that each child has specific, unique angels assigned to them. Until we realize that we have personal angels we won't take note of the benefits that they bring into our midst. Let's unpack a high profile example of personal angels at work from the book of Acts. Peter had been thrown in jail for proclaiming the gospel, the church went into prayer-mode, and the angelic broke loose:

> "And behold, an angel of the Lord stood next to him, and a light shone in the cell." (Acts 12:7)

Notice, a light shone. As we've discussed in the previous chapters, manifestations of light and heat often accompany angelic visitation. Now, Satan masquerades as an angel of light (see 2 Corinthians 11:14). So if Satan attempts to act as an angel of light, then it must mean that heavenly angels are authentic beings of light. James also referenced God as being the Father of Lights (see James 1:17). Recognizing these characteristics will equip you to spot angelic activity in your own personal life.

So after this angel wakes Peter up and breaks him out of jail, Peter then makes his way to the house of Mary where other believers are waiting:

> "When he realized this, he went to the house of Mary, the mother of John whose other name was Mark, where many were gathered together and were praying. And when he

knocked at the door of the gateway, a servant girl named Rhoda came to answer. Recognizing Peter's voice, in her joy she did not open the gate but ran in and reported that Peter was standing at the gate. They said to her, 'You are out of your mind." But she kept insisting that it was so, and they kept saying, 'It is his angel!'" (Acts 12:12-15)

She was absolutely sure that she saw Peter. Yet when reporting it to the crew, they said, "It is his angel!" This reveals a hidden truth to us: angelic activity was so common in the early church that without further investigation, they posited that what Rhoda saw was his angel. This should tell us something about how common the angelic should be for us. Not only that, they said his angel. They didn't say, "It's an angel!" They said his angel. This points to a personal spirit.

You might wonder, why did they think the angel looked like Peter? Often, your personal angel will take on your image. They are so invested in your calling and purpose that they will take on characteristics of you as a person. Often times, people will see the angel of someone they know and misdiagnose it as an example of bilocation. Now, I believe in bi-location and that a person can be in two places at once. In fact, I have been told that folks have seen me in places and regions where I wasn't physically. Yet, many times it's simply a person's angel that is manifesting in another area and people attribute such things to bi-location. This might be heavy for some of you or a little "out there" so to speak. Yet, keep in mind that God is supernatural.

ZECHARIAH'S ANGEL

The prophet Zechariah had continual encounters with a specific angel in the Word. In fact, we see that he hasn't yet discovered the name of his angel but he does refer to this being in a unique way repeatedly throughout his writing. He continually says, "The angel of the Lord who talked to me said..."In fact, he references this angel 16 times in the first 6 chapters of his short prophetic book.

It's very apparent that Zechariah had a specific and unique personal angel that assisted him in his prophetic exploits. Not only that, but he regularly interacted with the angel and was familiar with the angel's way of communicating. He linked the angel with speaking. Normally, we link angels with abstract celestial ideas that can't be put into words yet Zechariah had a practical look at the angel in his life.

We are called to run with angels. In so doing, they'll bolster our walk with Jesus and give assistance where needed. Learn to become familiar with your personal angels and how you can cooperate with their specific function in your life. When you do, you'll see more vividly and hear more clearly.

CHURCH & WATCHER ANGELS

CONGREGATIONAL & GOVERNMENTAL ASSIGNMENTS

THERE ARE ANGELS ASSIGNED TO CHURCHES. THIS IS VITAL information for pastors, church leaders, deacons and elders. Why is it important to know this? Because oftentimes, churches have a certain slant in their ministry. In other words, a churches DNA contains specific callings, outreaches and focuses.

For some churches it might be giving shelter to the homeless. To another church it is raising up entrepreneurial leaders. For another church it could be marriage and family. Many people don't realize this.

We have a big problem in the body of Christ and it's that we look at other churches and ministries and say, "They shouldn't focus so much on this," or "They spend too much time emphasizing that." What we don't realize is that the body of Christ as a whole offers varying, unique giftings and focus. If everyone did the same thing, Christ's bride would be incomplete.

You see this play out in the seven churches in the book of Revelation. They all vary in strengths and weaknesses. The hand is not the foot and the foot is not the hand. All parts of the body serve various functions. The angelic realm helps with facilitating these unique ministries. Along with unique callings are unique angels over God's house.

JOHN'S ASCENSION

In the book of Revelation, we see God breaking the traditional order of angelic rank through an encounter with John. Normally, as we've discussed, God is in heaven at the top of the ladder, angels mediate, and we are at the bottom.

One day, we will ascend and judge angels, but for now we are a little lower than them. Yet in this instance, we see John actually ascending beyond the angelic realm and having direct communication with God. From there, John writes to the angels of these churches, commissioning them to give words to the church they are assigned to assist.

This might be the only times we see this natural order switched up in Scripture and it's beautiful. God says to John repeatedly:

- "To the angel of the church in **Ephesus** write..." (Revelation 2:1)
- "To the angel of the church in **Smyrna** write..." (Revelation 2:8)
- "To the angel of the church in **Pergamum** write..." (Revelation 2:12)

- "To the angel of the church in **Thyatira** write..." (Revelation 2:18)
- "To the angel of the church in **Sardis** write..." (Revelation 3:1)
- "To the angel of the church in **Philadelphia** write..." (Revelation 3:7)
- "To the angel of the church in **Laodicea** write..." (Revelation 3:7)

The order was swapped and John became a messenger to angels rather than receiving messages from angels. But take note, each church in each region had a specific angel assigned. Not only that, but as you study these passages in the second and third chapter of Revelation, you will see that these churches had unique functions. Some of the churches receive rebuke, others receive encouragement. Not all churches are the same. Diversity of angels accompany the diversities of church callings.

Spend time with the Lord discovering the unique angels over your church. Beckon God's insight in learning to cooperate with their function. Don't neglect the heavenly beings over the congregation. Many in and around church cultures are only mindful of God and people. Yet there is a third force at play. God's arsenal is vast. Your church is not without the help, assistance, protection, and insight given by God's angelic beings.

~

WATCHER ANGELS

IN THE SAME WAY THAT ANGELS ARE ASSIGNED TO CHURCHES, other angels are assigned to governments. Watchers are high level angels that oversee the rise and fall of leaders. They are celestial beings that are strictly assigned to watching over governments. They fill a massive role in the earth. Think of all of the impacts, both good and bad, that world leaders have had throughout the centuries. Watchers oversee this activity and likely report what is happening among angelic ranks. We see their function clearly throughout the fourth chapter of Daniel.

> "I saw in the visions of my head as I lay in bed, and behold, a **watcher**, a holy one, came down from heaven." (Daniel 4:13 emphasis added)

> "The sentence is by the decree of the **watchers**, the decision by the word of the holy ones, to the end that the living may know that the Most High rules the kingdom of men and gives it to whom he will and sets over it the lowliest of men." (Daniel 4:17 emphasis added)

> "And because the king saw a **watcher**, a holy one, coming down from heaven and saying, 'Chop down the tree and destroy it, but leave the stump of its roots in the earth, bound with a band of iron and bronze, in the tender grass of the field, and let him be wet with the dew of heaven, and let his portion be with the beasts of the field, till seven

periods of time pass over him.'" (Daniel 4:23 emphasis added)

These "holy ones" are very governmentally minded. They not only oversee facets of world leadership but they also speak into these arenas like we see in the 23rd verse above. Without these watchers in place, governmental structure around the world would be lacking. We often think that everything is left up to the vote of a ballot but God has angels in places and positions in order to work out His will. Whether it's church government or world government, the angelic is not absent.

5

HEALING ANGELS

DIVINE MINISTERS OF HEALTH

"For an angel went down at a certain time into the pool and stirred up the water; then whoever stepped in first, after the stirring of the water, was made well of whatever disease he had." (John 5:4 NKJV)

THIS PASSAGE SPEAKS FOR ITSELF. AN ANGEL WAS ASSIGNED TO be proactive in assisting with means and methods of healing. Angels are organized in these things. It says, "at a certain time." In other words, there was a consistent protocol, order and schedule for these matters. God had set up a supernatural reservoir, so to speak, to bring about healing. Yet the water in the pool wasn't full of healing anointing until the angelic was involved.

In meetings, in homes, or on the street—angels still give assistance in healing grace. In fact, this isn't the only time that we see the angelic giving aid in the arena of healing. One could argue that Elijah's confrontation with Jezebel left him in need of a serious emotional healing. Remember, healing purchased by Jesus is not merely for the body. It includes the mind, the emotions, relationships, finances, family and more. It's total redemption on every level of life.

"And he lay down and slept under a broom tree. And behold, an angel touched him and said to him, 'Arise and eat.' And he looked, and behold, there was at his head a cake baked on hot stones and a jar of water. And he ate and drank and lay down again. And the angel of the Lord came again a second time and touched him and said, 'Arise and eat, for the journey is too great for you.' And he arose and ate and drank, and went in the strength of that food forty days and forty nights to Horeb, the mount of God." (1 Kings 19:5-8)

Elijah was in a bad place. He went from the pinnacle of ministry success to wanting to die because of a woman named Jezebel. The angel supernaturally brought and baked food. He also brought water. Elijah took a nap. Then an angel brought more food. The food was of supernatural substance. How do we know that? Because Elijah ran on that substance for 40 days! The angel was God's choice to bring about supernatural strengthening and emotional wholeness after contention with Jezebel. This isn't the only type of angelic catering that exists in life.

We have a dear ministry friend named Gary Oates who sees into the angelic like very few people that I know. When ministering alongside him, there are certain points in the service in which he is no longer there, in a sense. He sort of disconnects and is looking past the crowds, past the natural, and into the spirit. From there, he will begin calling things out and bringing the instruction from the angelic realm into the room.

In one meeting, he saw an angel breathing fire on a person's head. He said to the person, "Your head is getting hot, isn't it?" The man replied that it was indeed getting hot. Gary knew that the man needed healing. It turned out, the man had a brain tumor and upon the encounter, he was instantly and miraculously healed. What was at work? A healing angel. You might think, isn't it the blood of Jesus that provides healing? What does the angel have to do with it?

Without question, the blood of Jesus is what paid for our healing. We are not taking from that whatsoever. The blood of Christ purchased our healing yet the methods of healing can vary greatly. Christ Himself healed with His own saliva on one day and then healed by simply speaking the Word another day. Oftentimes, angelic influence will be implemented to bring about healing and wholeness. As we become familiar with these varying methods, we become more apt to appropriate them properly.

6

REGIONAL & WARRING ANGELS

SPECIFIC PLACES & UNIQUE BATTLES

WE SEE FROM AREAS OF SCRIPTURE LIKE DANIEL 10 AND Ephesians 6 that there is a certain rank and order established in the angelic realms and the demonic realms alike. The demonic realm is a knock-off version of God's order. The Bible says, "Therefore let us be grateful for receiving a kingdom that **cannot be shaken**" (Hebrews 12:28 emphasis added).

See, the kingdom of darkness can be shaken in any way you can imagine. Yet the kingdom of heaven cannot be. We stand in an indestructible domain. While rankings and orders and regional assignments exist on both sides—the dark side is ultimately inferior in every way. Daniel's encounter with the angelic gives us clues on these principles:

"In those days I, Daniel, was mourning for three weeks. I ate no delicacies, no meat or wine entered my mouth, nor did I anoint myself at all, for the full three weeks. On the twenty-fourth day of the first month, as I was standing on the bank of the great river (that is, the Tigris) I lifted up my eyes and looked, and behold, a man clothed in linen, with a belt of fine gold from Uphaz around his waist." (Daniel 10:2-5)

Essentially, during the original Daniel fast, Daniel has a visitation from an angel. The angel goes on to provide insight on the battle that was taking place in the spirit:

"Then he said to me, "Fear not, Daniel, for from the first day that you set your heart to understand and humbled yourself before your God, your words have been heard, and I have come because of your words. The prince of the kingdom of Persia withstood me twenty-one days, but Michael, one of the chief princes, came to help me, for I was left there with the kings of Persia, and came to make you understand what is to happen to your people in the latter days. For the vision is for days yet to come." (Daniel 10:12-14)

Within this domain, angelic beings have assorted facets, functions, rankings and regions. Notice, there is a dark angel known as the prince of the kingdom of Persia. This angel was assigned over a specific region. Under him would have been lower and lesser demons and foul spirits at work. Yet God answers this stronghold by sending a warring angel to do battle. The archangel Michael comes on the scene and fights this principality in order to see to it that Daniel's prayer was answered and manifested.

Take note, Gabriel was being withstood as a messenger angel. Michael is a warring angel who came to fight and take care of battle oriented business. Even in the book of Jude we see a similar event described, "But when the archangel Michael, contending with the devil, was disputing about the body of Moses, he did not presume to pronounce a blasphemous judgment, but said, 'The Lord rebuke you'" (Jude 1:9).

Michael knew the protocol and did not pronounce, "I rebuke you," but instead cited the name of the Lord, the ultimate authority. These battles are very real and spiritual warfare is very real. This is why it's important to not flippantly throw around spiritual warfare and go around stirring up fights with devils that God has not called you to. These things are dangerous. We want to fight from and out of a place of intimately loving and knowing Jesus.

Back to Daniel: the fact is, Daniel's prayer was answered the first day that he prayed. Yet a delay took place because of a fight in heaven. Should you experience a delay, know that the angelic is fighting on your behalf to see about a manifestation of God's promise and word.

Why does any of this matter? Why does God care to teach us about regional demons and angels? Here's why: many of you are called to specific regions that have specific strongholds. When you understand this, you know how to move forward to effectively win your region for the glory of God. There are national angels, state governing angels and more specific regional angels. Partnering with the angelic forces in your region will ensure a more effective influence and experience in this earth.

WARRING ANGELS

Angelic realms do battle. That's no secret. We often see conquering, warring, and battling angels depicted in art and in pop culture. The root of these depictions is indeed Biblical. Some angels have specific assignments to do battle here in the earth. Look at this example in the life of Elisha:

"He said, 'Do not be afraid, for those who are with us are more than those who are with them.' Then Elisha prayed and said, 'O Lord, please open his eyes that he may see.' So the Lord opened the eyes of the young man, and he saw, and behold, the mountain was full of horses and chariots of fire all around Elisha. And when the Syrians came down against him, Elisha prayed to the Lord and said, 'Please strike this people with blindness.' So he struck them with blindness in accordance with the prayer of Elisha. And Elisha said to them, 'This is not the way, and this is not the city. Follow me, and I will bring you to the man whom you seek.' And he led them to Samaria." (2 Kings 6:16-19)

Let's make this clear, Elisha prayed to God and God sent angels to strike the enemy with blindness. Elisha didn't pray to angels. We don't pray to angels. We pray to the Lord and it's the angels that bid to do the Lord's will! This is a very important distinguishing factor.

Note how it was warring angels that assisted in this battle. Elisha prayed that the man would have open eyes to be able to see that there were more beings in the spirit fighting for him than those who were against him. The warring angels in our midst outnumber those that are fighting against us.

> "For we do not wrestle against flesh and blood, but against the rulers, against the authorities, against the cosmic powers over this present darkness, against the spiritual forces of evil in the heavenly places." (Ephesians 6:12)

Elisha didn't say, "Alright. Let's go fight." Then proceed to draw a sword and do a bunch of flesh and blood battle. He understood the spiritual side of the battle. He saw what others did not. His eyes were opened. May our eyes be opened to see and understand that heaven's angelic hosts are greater both in quality, authority, and quantity than that of the kingdom of darkness.

7

SERAPHIM & CHERUBIM ANGELS

RESIDENTS OF THE THRONE ROOM

WHILE DISCUSSING THE TOPIC OF ANGELS, I DON'T WANT TO leave out the seraphim and cherubim that we see in Scripture. They aren't necessarily the primary avenue of angelic influence in our lives, however, in order to make this teaching more exhaustive—they're worth bringing up.

The Hebrew word for seraphim means burning ones. The seraphim in heaven fly above the throne of God. We see this in the book of Isaiah which says, "In the year that King Uzziah died I saw the Lord sitting upon a throne, high and lifted up; and the train of his robe filled the temple. **Above him** stood the seraphim. Each had six wings: with two he covered his face, and with two he covered his feet, and with two he flew" (Isaiah 6:1-2 emphasis added).

These burning ones convey and protect holiness. They have an assignment to purge and refine. If you continue in Isaiah, the text says, "And I said: 'Woe is me! For I am lost; for I am a man of unclean lips, and I dwell in the midst of a people of unclean lips; for my eyes have seen the King, the Lord of hosts!' Then one of the seraphim flew to me, having in his hand a burning coal that he had taken with tongs from the altar. And he touched my mouth and said: 'Behold, this has touched your lips; your guilt is taken away, and your sin atoned for'" (Isaiah 6:5-7).

The cherubim, however, are around the throne of God. "And before the throne there was as it were a sea of glass, like crystal. And around the throne, on each side of the throne, are four living creatures, full of eyes in front and behind: the first living creature like a lion, the second living creature like an ox, the third living creature with the face of a man, and the fourth living creature like an eagle in flight. And the four living creatures, each of them with six wings, are full of eyes all around and within, and day and night they never cease to say, 'Holy, holy, holy, is the Lord God Almighty, who was and is and is to come!'" (Revelation 4:6-7).

I will say, there is some debate over whether or not these living creatures in revelation are cherubim or not. However, when we look at Ezekiel, he encounters four living creatures and later describes them in the tenth chapter as having a cherubim sort of face (see Ezekiel 10:14).

These types of angels exist primarily on the heavenly side of things. Most of the angels that we unpack in this book are working in and throughout the earth the seraphim and cherubim are in the throne room of God. Like Isaiah, encountering them is still a possibility and we should go after it all. If it's in the Bible, it's ours to chase. One thing I will say, is that these cherubim are described as having multiple eyes in the book of revelation. In fact, they have eyes all around their heads. This speaks of their seer nature.

In the angelic, there is a revelatory element. You are able to see things that you couldn't before. Angels are look out over the earth with eyes that we don't have. They witness things we don't see and they give things that we don't have. The angelic is a deep realm but one we should access in every way, shape, and form because there exists resources that we lack. Whether the angels are heaven-side or earth-side, our study of them and relationship with them is key in the Kingdom.

8

JUDGMENT ANGELS

THE SEVERITY OF ANGELIC FUNCTION

THIS IS NOT NECESSARILY A HAPPY TOPIC FOR MOST. YET THE judgment of God for the believer is a blessing. We've been spared from God's wrath and judgment. Yet judgment still exists in varying capacities and it's important to discover how the angelic participates in this function of God's nature. Judgment is so important. Basically, if you stand before a judge and the judgment is wrong—goodness cannot prevail. God's judgments are perfect, pure and holy. As a result, love and goodness prevail.

It's true that Jesus said that He did not come to judge the earth. That's true. Yet it doesn't mean that God never judges. It just means it isn't what He came for. It wasn't His first response or go-to option. His intention is mercy, not judgment. Yet judgment exists. We see this both in the Old Testament and the New Testament, which we'll read shortly. Many have misconceptions about God's nature. They believe that God somehow changed in between the Old Testament and the New. Yet this isn't the case. He is the same yesterday, today and forever. What changed was how God began to deal with man according to Christ's blood at Calvary.

We now have a greater access point through the veil by way of the blood of Christ Jesus. It's not that God changed but the sacrifice altered how God deals with man. Yet His nature remains the same and judgment is still a part of God's nature. Paul said, "Note then the kindness and the severity of God: severity toward those who have fallen, but God's kindness to you, provided you continue in his kindness. Otherwise you too will be cut off" (Romans 11:22).

Judgment might seem harsh or wrong in our finite thinking, yet we have to examine things through a holistic lens. In eternity, everything that God does will make sense. Even if things look bad, off, or wrong now—God is working things out for ultimate good. The beautiful thing is, as we are aligned with Him, we don't have to worry about judgment. Let's examine how the angelic interacts in the arena of judgment:

> "He let loose on them his burning anger, wrath, indignation, and distress, a company of destroying angels." (Psalm 78:49)

> "And that night the angel of the LORD went out and struck down 185,000 in the camp of the Assyrians. And when people arose early in the morning, behold, these were all dead bodies." (2 Kings 19:35)

"Let their way be dark and slippery, with the angel of the Lord pursuing them!" (Psalm 35:6)

"For we are about to destroy this place, because the outcry against its people has become great before the Lord, and the Lord has sent us to destroy it." (Genesis 19:13)

Who was speaking in this passage? Angels. Not angels of darkness but angels from God. We've got to either believe the whole Bible or not believe any of the Bible. It isn't pick and choose. These passages don't mean that God is trigger-happy and ready to judge at the drop of a hat. In fact, He is slow to anger. He abounds in loving kindness. If a judgment happens, you can bet that God has been patient for a long, long time.

This isn't to create or spur a fear of punishment in you either. You could make 400 mistakes in a day and God would still be so proud of you. He loves you so deeply and unconditionally. He is the best loving Father. When we look at verses on judgment, it is important to keep this in mind. We have got to know that mercy is His default position, judgment is the exception. Otherwise, we'll live afraid in an unhealthy way.

Angels are simply tools in the hand of God to carry out certain judgments in the earth. They don't generate judgment by their own choosing. They don't carry out wrath apart from the will of God. You might think, well that is all Old Testament. The New Covenant doesn't contain this stuff.

In fact, judgment is found in the New Testament. We see it take place even after Christ's sacrifice.

"Now when day came, there was no little disturbance among the soldiers over what had become of Peter. And after Herod searched for him and did not find him, he examined the sentries and ordered that they should be put to death. Then he went down from Judea to Caesarea and spent time there.

Now Herod was angry with the people of Tyre and Sidon, and they came to him with one accord, and having persuaded Blastus, the king's chamberlain, they asked for peace, because their country depended on the king's country for food. On an appointed day Herod put on his royal robes, took his seat upon the throne, and delivered an oration to them.

And the people were shouting, 'The voice of a god, and not of a man!' Immediately an angel of the Lord struck him down, because he did not give God the glory, and he was eaten by worms and breathed his last." (Acts 12:18-23)

Herod was essentially pretending to be God. He had no fear of God. He pompously delivered a great speech and people thought He was the voice of God. Instead of giving God credit, he took the credit and it cost him his life. It was an example of New Covenant judgment, carried out by an angel.

"After this I saw **four angels** standing at the four corners of the earth, holding back the four winds of the earth, that no wind might blow on earth or sea or against any tree. Then I saw another angel ascending from the rising of the sun, with the seal of the living God, and he called with a loud voice to the four angels who **had been given power to harm the earth and sea.**" (Revelation 7:1-2 emphasis added)

These are shakings that take place. These are glimpses of judgment brought forth by angels. Often, we want to get stuck in "happy-land." And look, the Kingdom is extremely happy. Yet we ought not blind ourselves to judgment. It's key that we know how God moves. Even if we ourselves are not experiencing judgment personally, we should know about it and how God uses it.

"It was also about these that Enoch, the seventh from Adam, prophesied, saying, "Behold, the Lord comes with ten thousands of His holy ones, to execute judgment on all and to convict all the ungodly of all their deeds of ungodliness that they have committed in such an ungodly way, and of all the harsh things that ungodly sinners have spoken against Him." These are grumblers, malcontents, following their own sinful desires; they are loud-mouthed boasters, showing favoritism to gain advantage." (Jude 1:14-16)

Here, the writer Jude references the book of Enoch. Now, this book is not a part of the canonized Scripture and should not be esteemed as such, yet it was influential and credible enough to be mentioned in the Word. If you dig into the book of Enoch, you'll find that Enoch talks much of the angelic realm, even giving names to various angels and providing interesting insight. In this particular mention, Enoch prophesied that the Lord will come in the end times to execute judgment. How so? By bringing ten thousand of His holy ones...angels.

See, when a nation is in sin, it hinders the blessing of God from flowing freely. The misalignment puts a damper on God's favor and abundance in the land. Now, regions and pockets within the nation can be blessed when God has His remnant there—yet when a national acknowledgment of Jesus is lacking, blessing dries up. When a nation has turned against God, protection lifts. That's why we must pray for our nation to see these things turned around. It's on the church's shoulders to pray for radical change in a nation.

Here are a couple of examples: in Norway, there was recently a lightning bolt that struck 323 reindeer on the spot. It was an entire herd. A day later, a lightning bolt hit in Texas and 19 cattle were killed. You might think, what does this have to do with anything? Well the Scripture says, "He gave over their cattle to the hail and their flocks to thunderbolts. He let loose on them His burning anger, wrath, indignation, and distress, a company of destroying angels" (Psalm 78:48-49). I'm not bashing Norway, Texas or any other place, however there are times when judgment happens and a divine alignment is needed and God can use varying methods to bring this about.

I was in Columbia ministering. The first night there I was lying on my bed seeking the Lord prior to going into a crusade. As I was there, my spiritual eyes were opened and I saw an angel walk up from behind me. The angel approached and spoke to me in a parable. The angel spoke about judgment coming to the nation and a shaking in the ground occurring. I don't remember the exact phrasing but the parable spoke of an earthquake that was tied to national sin. The devil was not there nor was he a part of it. Many people think that because Jesus rebuked the storm that all natural disasters are of the devil but that isn't biblical.

I went from that encounter into meetings and preached about it. I spoke on our need to cry out to God in repentance to see the earthquake thwarted and God's judgment to relent. Sure enough, that day an earthquake hit. Fortunately, it hit in the ocean and not on the mainland. It was a sign of a shaking and of the earth's groaning for the sons of God to be revealed. Oftentimes these events will hit in the hub of a nation as a sign to the people in it.

I was in Montana preaching once and in a meeting I saw a vision in which Jesus had a fan in His hand and was waving it over the congregation. It speaks of holiness. When you harvest wheat, you blow wind to get the chaff out. Later that day, extremely high powered winds came in a very destructive way. They snapped poles, took down power lines and more. That same day some sexual allegations against a high profile college coach in the area were exposed to be true. Many don't know this side of God yet the Lord cares dearly about the state of a region's purity. He wants to purge the threshing floor to separate the wheat from the chaff.

One other quick example. I was having my morning coffee and waiting on the Lord. I set my coffee down on the table next to me. When I looked back at it, the coffee had supernaturally moved. I sensed that it was an angelic movement to get my attention. It was sitting on top of the remote to my fan and was on the verge of spilling out. I instantly remembered Jeremiah 1:13 which says, "The word of the Lord came to me a second time, saying, 'What do you see?' And I said, 'I see a boiling pot, facing away from the north.'" From there the verse goes on to describe the boiling pot being God's judgment about to be poured out for national sin. Not only that, but I knew that because the coffee was sitting on my fan control that the judgment would involve whirlwinds. Well that very day, there were somewhere around 70 whirlwinds that broke out in the heart of America.

Judgments shake a region in order to convict and turn back those regions. Judgment is never an end in itself but a means to an end. The end, of course, is people turning back to God. You can't separate the goodness of God and the judgment of God. They are all operations of the Kingdom. When we align our lives with heaven, we aren't the recipients of judgment but of grace, revelation, wisdom and insight. Yet to do the teaching justice, it must be mentioned that the angelic does bring about assistance in the area of judgment in the earth.

9

MESSENGER ANGELS

GOD'S CHOSEN COMMUNICATORS

"Therefore we must pay much closer attention to what we have heard, lest we drift away from it. For since **the message declared by angels proved to be reliable**, and every transgression or disobedience received a just retribution..." (Hebrews 2:1-2 emphasis added).

THE WRITER OF HEBREWS IS BASICALLY VALIDATING THE message that angels carry and the reality that they do indeed carry messages. People are really quick to reference scriptures about not worshipping angels or the elect being deceived and as a result, they don't consider angels an avenue for enlightenment whatsoever.

As a result, they miss out on one of God's chosen relays. Paul, the writer who warned of deception in spirituality without Christ, also spoke heavily on visions, experiences, and encounters with the angelic in the spirit realm. A balanced approach has got to be taken concerning these matters.

Throughout the scriptures, we see that Gabriel's mode of operation is messaging. He is a communicating angel. This means revelation, insight, and understanding. Let's have an expository look at this playing out in the book of Daniel:

"When I, Daniel, had seen the vision, I sought to understand it." (Daniel 8:15)

Before going any further, I want to point you to the second part of this sentence. Daniel sought to understand his vision. He leaned in. He didn't merely have the vision. He sought understanding. Many have visions from God that are genuine and they immediately want to spout about it to everyone, yet they haven't taken the time to chase understanding regarding what was shown and seen. It is the understanding of the vision that bears fruit. Let's continue:

"And behold, there stood before me one having the appearance of a man. And I heard a man's voice between the banks of the Ulai, and it called, 'Gabriel, make this man understand the vision.' So He came near where I stood. And when He came, I was frightened and fell on my face. But He said to me, 'Understand, O son of man, that the vision is for the time of the end.'

And when He had spoken to me, I fell into a deep sleep with my face to the ground. But He touched me and made me stand up. He said, 'Behold, I will make known to you what shall be at the latter end of the indignation, for it refers to the appointed time of the end.'" (Daniel 8:15-19)

As Daniel leaned in, revelation came. It came in the form of Gabriel appearing and unpacking things that were futuristic and prophetic. This is the nature of the gospel: conveying messages. When a messenger shows up, they can deliver key insights that change your destiny in radical ways. A messenger angel will provide glimpses, insights, warnings, revelation, timelines, instructions, and commissionings that cause your life to do a total one-eighty.

SPECIFICITY

After Daniel had received revelation from the messenger Gabriel, he encountered him again in the next chapter:

"...while I was speaking in prayer, the man Gabriel, whom I had seen in the vision at the first, came to me in swift flight at the time of the evening sacrifice. He made me understand, speaking with me and saying, 'O Daniel, I have now come out to give you insight and understanding. At the beginning of your pleas for mercy a word went out, and I have come to tell it to you, for you are greatly loved. Therefore consider the word and understand the vision.'" (Daniel 9:21-23)

Now Daniel recognizes Gabriel and calls him by name. He became increasingly familiar with and aware of the angelic—something we are all called to. Take note that in this passage it says that Gabriel came "in swift flight." Some argue over the appearance of angels. Do they have wings or not? Are they tall or short? Do they look like humans or do they look like some other celestial being? The reality is, they're all different and each respective angel can manifest differently depending on what is needed.

Some angels in Scripture are massive, glorified beings that cause humans to drop on their face. Yet we also see the scriptures saying, "Do not forget to entertain strangers, for by so doing some have unwittingly entertained angels" (Hebrews 13:2 NKJV). In other words, you could be encountering an angelic being without even realizing it due to an uncanny human-like form. These are truths to keep in mind when unpacking these passages.

Notice that words that continue to come up in the Daniel 9 passage is understanding and insight. This is the bedrock of a messenger angel. Their messages are always consequential to you and often many people around you. We see messenger angels appearing in the New Testament as well:

"And there appeared to him an angel of the Lord standing on the right side of the altar of incense. And Zechariah was troubled when he saw him, and fear fell upon him. But the angel said to him, 'Do not be afraid, Zechariah, for your prayer has been heard, and your wife Elizabeth will bear you a son, and you shall call his name John. And you will have joy and gladness, and many will rejoice at his birth, for he will be great before the Lord. And he must not drink wine or strong drink, and he will be filled with the Holy Spirit, even from his mother's womb. And he will turn many of the children of Israel to the Lord their God, and he will go before Him in the spirit and power of Elijah, to turn the hearts of the fathers to the children, and the disobedient to the wisdom of the just, to make ready for the Lord a people prepared.'" (Luke 1:11-17)

Notice how specific this messenger's dialog was with Zechariah. The encounter shaped a destiny. He spoke about him, his wife, and his son. He gave insight into his son's lifestyle and task for the decades to come. He spoke about intergenerational ministry and his job as a trailblazer for the Christ. It doesn't get much more specific. Why is this so specific? Because it was angelic. When angels come with messages, they are crystal clear. See, Paul said, "We know in part and we prophesy in part," in 1 Corinthians 13:9. So when dreams and visions occur, it can be hazy. Sometimes it requires an interpretation. Often we might not be certain if we heard God correctly so we will bounce it off a trusted brother or sister.

For example, Daniel, Shadrach, Meshach and Abed-nego were all given interpretive ability. The Word says they had, "all wisdom, endowed with knowledge, understanding learning, and competent to stand in the king's palace, and to teach them the literature and language of the Chaldeans" (Daniel 1:4). Yet Daniel had a special gift to accurately interpret dreams as we see later, "There is a man in your kingdom in whom is the spirit of the holy gods. In the days of your father, light and understanding and wisdom like the wisdom of the gods were found in him, and King Nebuchadnezzar, your father—your father the king—made him chief of the magicians, enchanters, Chaldeans, and astrologers, because an excellent spirit, knowledge, and understanding to interpret dreams, explain riddles, and solve problems were found in this Daniel, whom the king named Belteshazzar. Now let Daniel be called, and he will show the interpretation" (Daniel 5:11-12).

We all, as believers, have the Spirit of God and can interpret visions and dreams. Anyone can identify colors, numbers, and symbols within dreams and leverage a balanced dream interpretation structure to help discover God's message. Yet some carry a special anointing to do so. Why do I bring all of this up? Because when a messenger angel appears—these special anointings, or gifts, are not necessary whatsoever. A messenger angel makes things crystal clear. There is no seeing or hearing dimly or in part.

When things are so weighty and consequential that God cannot risk losing His message in murky waters—He will send a messenger angel. It could happen while awake or asleep. We see this in Matthew 2:13, "Now when they had departed, behold, an angel of the Lord appeared to Joseph in a dream and said, "Rise, take the child and his mother, and flee to Egypt, and remain there until I tell you, for Herod is about to search for the child, to destroy him." Obviously, this was far too consequential to send a parabolic vision that required days to search out and interpret. During the spread of the gospel in the early church, messenger angels played an integral role:

> "But the high priest rose up, and all who were with him (that is, the party of the Sadducees), and filled with jealousy they arrested the apostles and put them in the public prison. But during the night an angel of the Lord opened the prison doors and brought them out, and said, 'Go and stand in the temple and speak to the people all the words of this Life.' And when they heard this, they entered the temple at daybreak and began to teach." (Acts 5:17-21)

This angel didn't merely break them free, but delivered a needed message. Interestingly enough, this angel told them to go to a very, very public place and begin teaching. Persecution was hot, the church was under a microscope, and rather than telling them to hide away in house churches— he tells them to preach openly. Angels will often tell you things that are counterintuitive. They'll tell you to do things that you might not believe came from God had you just seen it in a blurry vision.

We see another messenger speaking to Phillip a few chapters later, "Now an angel of the Lord said to Philip, 'Rise and go toward the south to the road that goes down from Jerusalem to Gaza.' This is a desert place" (Acts 8:26). Bear in mind, this is after the Holy Ghost was poured out. Despite this new direct connection with the Spirit of God, God still chose to use angels as regular messengers. These message deliveries via angels are littered throughout the book of Acts. How much more is this needed today?

PERSONAL ENCOUNTERS

I once had a messenger angel appear to me the night before preaching a three day conference. The angel spoke to me and told me to have a commissioning service the first night and that a woman at the service would be involved. This is counterintuitive. Why? Because standard protocol for these conferences is to teach and build up for two days and then on the third day and final service, you do a commissioning service with the laying on of hands.

I went ahead and did a commissioning service the next night. A lady approached at the altar call and sure enough, she was ready to be moved and released into a new season of life and ministry and it turned out, this was the only service that she could make. God sent an angel with an urgent message and disrupted protocol in order for her to get what God had for her.

Another time I was preaching near Chicago. I went to sleep the night before a meeting that was scheduled for the next morning. I was awakened by a wing or a wind that brushed along my forehead. I've found that when God touches my forehead in an encounter it often involves foreknowledge and foresight. I checked the clock and it was 10:38 p.m. I knew this was a sign pointing to Acts 10:38 which says, "...how God anointed Jesus of Nazareth with the Holy Spirit and with power. He went about doing good and healing all who were oppressed by the devil, for God was with him." As a result, I knew I was to have a healing service the next morning.

The morning came and I asked the host what the wifi password was to his house. He said, "Acts 10:38." The Word of the Lord was clear. During the meeting we saw deaf ears popping open, shoulders being restored, and healing manifesting powerfully. God's presence to heal was there in a remarkable way. It was through angelic wind that this chain of events began!

Messenger angels are so prevalent in the Word and ought to be so prevalent in our lives. This means of revelation and encounter can provide such a needed depth of insight and understanding into our lives. Learn to open and avail yourself to these things. They are all directed by and orchestrated by the Holy Spirit and they all point us closer to Jesus—something we could all use a little more of.

10

ANGELIC WONDERS

MANIFESTATIONS FROM HEAVENLY HOSTS

I WANT TO TAKE SOME TIME TO CLOSE OUT THE BOOK WITH THE
topic of wonders. Yes, angels oversee regions and governments. Yes, angels provide messages. Yes, angels worship at
the throne and facilitate healing. Yet an area of the angelic
that can't go without mention is the area of wonders. Jesus
declared that signs and wonders would follow those that
believe, so we ought to expect them. God uses wonders to get
His message and/or purpose across. Angels often manifest
wonders in our midst and with this chapter I want to provide
some scriptural backing and many testimonies. Testimonies
trigger similar testimonies, so may the Lord manifest angelic
wonders in your midst.

The Bible says, "The secret things belong to the Lord our
God, but the things that are revealed belong to us and to our
children forever, that we may do all the words of this law"
(Deuteronomy 29:29). God often packages messages to us in
mysterious ways. Why? So that hunger is required to search

it out and experience it. "It is the glory of God to conceal things, but the glory of kings is to search things out" (Proverbs 25:2). When we unlock mystery, it belongs to us and our children forever. It's a revelation that can't be taken away. Signs and wonders can be mysterious yet within the mystery is revelation that is literally eternal and invaluable.

"And it shall come to pass afterward, that I will pour out my Spirit on all flesh; your sons and your daughters shall prophesy, your old men shall dream dreams, and your young men shall see visions. Even on the male and female servants in those days I will pour out my Spirit.

And I will show wonders in the heavens and on the earth, blood and fire and columns of smoke. The sun shall be turned to darkness, and the moon to blood, before the great and awesome day of the Lord comes. And it shall come to pass that everyone who calls on the name of the Lord shall be saved." (Joel 2:28-32)

Take note of the progression of manifestations. We go from outpouring to dreams, visions, wonders in the heavens, blood, fire and smoke. This is the glory of the Lord on earth. We know that the glory of God is covering the earth yet the Bible says that the, "Knowledge of the glory of the Lord shall cover the earth" (see Habakkuk 2:14). The glory is here...it's simply our knowledge of it that is being opened up. Angelic wonders are a means by which God is heightening our awareness of the knowledge of His glory in the earth.

GOD IS CALLING

I was preaching in Arizona and went to sleep in my hotel room the night before. I woke up to the sound of my hotel phone ringing. I answered the phone. It was a dead signal, no one was on the other line. I jotted it down and went back to sleep. I was in the meeting the next day and phones started going off in the meeting left and right. Angels do some wild stuff. One lady hopped up and grabbed her purse which contained the phone and ran out. An elder on the front row had their phone go off, and elders know not to have their phones on during service.

In fact, all of these people came up to me in between sessions and said, "So sorry. My phone was on silent—I don't know what happened." I told them not to worry about it and that it was a sign and wonder. Whenever I share this story around the world, it's a sure thing that phones begin going off. We've seen worship music start playing through phones, and ringtones that people didn't even have on their phone begin to play. We've seen people's phone, which was off, completely supernaturally turn on and begin to chime.

You might think, why would this happen? Here's why: every time we've seen that wonder manifest, it's been because God was calling these specific people and urging them to answer the call of God. Many of them had been dormant in what they were called to do and needed to answer God's call. Sometimes people love being in meetings and around the anointing yet when God begins speaking, prophesying and calling people to His will—people measure the cost and back away. They don't pick up the phone, so to speak. When we've had these things happen, we've seen ex-pastors re-commit to the ministry and many people come back to the call of God.

SUPERMAN

I was once in a meeting and Stacey Campbell was prophesying over me and as she kept saying, "Clark Kent. Clark Kent. You're Clark Kent." It wasn't spiritual to me at all. I could hardly hear her due to loud speakers and music but a friend who was with me heard it. Essentially she was saying that I was unassuming yet had unique supernatural power working with me. From that point on, I kept seeing this superman thing everywhere. It was following me. I went into a prophetic dream and was flying like Superman. It was glorious. I didn't want to leave the dream.

In it, God began to show me that Superman had pristine vision, and had ears to hear. He can hear someone calling for help from miles and miles away. He had power to do good and to assist. After God shared these various analogies with me, I woke up. I went to the bathroom and looked in the mirror and my hair was sort of down and I had a Clark Kent style curl on my forehead...just like Superman! It was humorous. Imagine an angel licking his thumb and doing up my hair to look like Superman. These small wonders build our faith, expectancy, and validate what God has been speaking.

During this season, I was locked away in prayer, waiting

on the Lord. This Superman thing meant a lot to me. The symbolism of supernatural power by God's grace ran deep in me. So much so that when I was at home, I kept the Superman theme song as my ringtone. (If I was in public I'd keep my phone on silent. A ringtone like that might make a guy seem a bit full of himself). Yet between God and I, I kept this ringtone at home. At the end of this 40 day fast and season of being locked away, The Lord had spoken to me specifically to attend a conference in Idaho. The title of the conference was, It's Time: Releasing Apostolic Power.

I had kept my phone on silent, as I was in these meetings all day and traveling. I woke up at 6:14 a.m. to the sound of my phone ringing...the Superman theme, of course. I knew my phone was on silent. I looked, and it was from an unknown caller. I answered and no one was there. I checked my phone and sure enough, it was set to silent. God supernaturally turned my volume on. I went to the restroom and looked in the mirror and I had a handprint in the middle of my chest. It was as if it was branded in my chest. I had to do a double take. It was right where the Superman logo would be. I knew something was up. This handprint stayed on my chest for an hour.

I sought God and the Lord began to show me Judges 6:14 which made sense given that I had woken up at 6:14 a.m. "And the Lord turned to him and said, 'Go in this might of yours and save Israel from the hand of Midian; do not I send you?'" I knew that it was an apostolic hour in which God was commissioning and sending His people. The word apostle actually means sent one. At this point, God was shifting my calling and destiny. He was sending me in a new way. Everything from the Stacey Campbell prophecy to the handprint, I knew God was sending me in a new way and all of these wonders worked to confirm this change.

MOVEMENTS AND MARKINGS

"Now when Herod was about to bring him out, on that very night, Peter was sleeping between two soldiers, bound with two chains, and sentries before the door were guarding the prison. And behold, an angel of the Lord stood next to him, and a light shone in the cell. He struck Peter on the side and woke him, saying, 'Get up quickly.'"

The two soldiers whom Peter was sleeping between didn't even notice what was happening. Angels have the ability to blind people to certain events happening around them, if needed.

"And the chains fell off his hands. And the angel said to him, 'Dress yourself and put on your sandals.' And he did so. And he said to him, 'Wrap your cloak around you and follow me.' And he went out and followed him. He did not know that what was being done by the angel was real, but thought he was seeing a vision. When they had passed the first and the second guard, they came to the iron gate leading into the city."

We see two powerful wonders here. First, the chains supernaturally fall off. A guard in this prison would have bound an inmate with heavy chains that were impossible to remove without a specific key. The angel doesn't even fool with the key. The chains just fall off. Secondly, they are walking through the facility, directly in front of guards who seemingly don't mind that they are leaving. Peter wasn't in a disguise. The angel didn't dress up as a guard and sneak Peter out of there in a duffle bag. They supernaturally walked out and God blinded the guards to what was happening.

> "It opened for them of its own accord, and they went out and went along one street, and immediately the angel left him. When Peter came to himself, he said, 'Now I am sure that the Lord has sent his angel and rescued me from the hand of Herod and from all that the Jewish people were expecting.'" (Acts 12:6-11)

What happened here? This massive iron gate that was the threshold of the city supernaturally opened. Angels have the ability to move objects, alter reality and shift things in a space, in ways that go beyond human ability or comprehension. We shouldn't be so confused by supernatural realities happening in our lives when we see how frequent they are in Scripture.

BEDTIME BASKETBALL

Several years ago I was putting my two kids to sleep. They were probably 4 and 6 at the time. My kids have always been very obedient and know that during bed time, they go to sleep and stay asleep. Things are regimented in that way and I've never had to have a bedtime struggle to keep the kids in bed. We just don't do that. As I was in my room I heard the basketball hit the basketball goal. I thought to myself, is Judah out of bed and shooting hoops? That's not gonna work. I went out, in father mode, and checked on the kids and both were completely sound asleep.

I went out and looked and the basketball was moving from where it had been shot. Nobody was out there. I took pictures, journaled it, recorded the day and time and went back to bed. I always want to find the wonder in these things. Angels don't do anything by chance or at random. They are super intentional and there is always meaning in these things.

Three months passed by. My son was getting bigger and we got him a new basketball goal. I set the old basketball goal by the door because I was going to throw it out. I was playing some ball with my son and as we are playing, I see a human arm. This might freak some of you out. It was a physical arm with my naked-eye in broad daylight. This arm swung out and pointed at the goal...the same goal that ball was shot on three months prior.

I wasn't thinking, Holy Ghost, revelation and encounter. I was thinking, who is in my house? I grabbed a rod that I had and went to investigate. As I went down the hall, I expected to have to clobber somebody. Sure enough, no one was there. It was angelic. There was something about this basketball goal.

I like to study how the Gregorian calendar (the calendar we use) meshes with the Hebrew calendar that Jesus used. Often, when something happens on the Hebrew calendar, three months later it will manifest on our Gregorian calendar. When I went back and meditated on this, the Lord showed me that the goal being shot by the angelic represented our calling to aim and hit the mark and climb higher in the things of God. What I was seeing was a fulfillment of this aim three months later. At the time in my life this symbolism was so, so important. It was spoken in a very childlike way, yet the Lord used this manifested wonder to declare something that I needed to hear.

HOMEWORK

I picked my kids up from school one day and we were headed to the grocery store. We were going down the interstate at about 75 miles per hour and I cracked the windows to get some fresh air. When I looked back my kids had a stunned look on their faces. Turns out, Judah was getting papers out of his backpack and his math homework got sucked out of the window. I apologized to him and let him know I would tell his teacher what had happened. There was no going back, as we were already miles down the road and traffic was crazy. By the time we would turn around and go back looking for it the wind probably would have taken it to who knows where.

We drove about ten more miles to the grocery store and got out. When I looked on the ground, I saw a piece of paper.

It had Judah's name on it with some math problems written down. I walked over to Judah and when he saw it his jaw hit the floor. It was his math homework. He said, "How did you do that?" I said, "I didn't do that. Angels did." Angels will work wonders in practical ways because God cares about the things that concern us.

Whether it's markings, manna, signs, wonders, messages, objects moving, or supernatural supply—angels are actively involved in our midst. I believe many people have angels at work among them without even being aware of it. My prayer is that you would gain a new knowledge of the glory of the Lord and that from here forward you would regularly interact with the angelic in your midst.

PRAYER FOR ANGELIC RELEASE

❧

Father, I pray that you would mark your people with angelic wonders, visitations, and habitations in a new way. Cause those reading this to understand the value and the necessity of angels in their lives. May they identify their personal angels, receive assistance from regional angels, gain insight from messenger angels, and be protected by warring angels who fight battles on their behalf, even while they sleep. Help us, Lord, to cooperate with the heavenly beings that you've released in our midst like never before, in Jesus' name, amen.

ABOUT THE AUTHOR

Brian Guerin is the founding president of Bridal Glory International. He graduated from the Brownsville School of Ministry/F.I.R.E. in 2001, and now travels throughout the U.S. and the world teaching and preaching the gospel of the Lord Jesus Christ. Brian has appeared on T.B.N. and GOD-TV and currently hosts his own broadcasting channel on YouTube. He also authored two previously released books, *Modern Day Mysticism* and *God of Wonders*. His main passion and emphasis in life is to draw the Bride of Christ into greater intimacy with the Bridegroom Himself-Jesus Christ, leading to the maturity of the Bride and the culmination of His glorious return. Brian also enjoys bringing great emphasis and depth to the art of hearing the voice of God through dreams, visions, signs, and wonders.

VISIT BRIDAL GLORY ON THE WEB & SOCIAL:
WWW.BRIDALGLORY.COM

SOCIAL: @BRIDALGLORY

FREE EXCERPT FROM
DIVINE ENCOUNTER

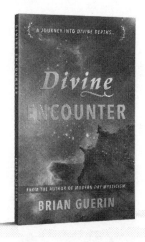

BY **BRIAN GUERIN**

*AVAILABLE AT **AMAZON.COM**

INTRODUCTION

My expectation with this book is that both while reading and after reading, you'll have run-ins with God you've never had before that will shift *everything*. My whole life up to this point has gone through this window—this vein of divine encounter, if you will. It's what we really long for and hunger for: to intimately *know Him* and *encounter Him*. Yet the encounter itself isn't the sole focus of our pursuit; what the encounter *produces* most importantly, is what we're going after—not just the *wow* of it all. What divine encounters produce is more important than the encounter itself.

Throughout this work, we'll be covering what many of these encounters are intended for, where they come from, and the various facets of their existence in our lives. I'm going to be dropping plenty of Scripture for a theological foundation, but I can tell you ahead of time, we'll also share plenty of stories, not just from the Scriptures, but from my personal life as we go.

Our aim is for this realm to break open into our world. That's how heaven works: the more you mull over, mediate, and turn your attention to certain aspects of the Kingdom, the more it opens up to touch us and flip our world upside down.

May the reality of an experiential God be yours as you work your way through these pages. Let the truths, principles, and stories within motivate and propel you into a place of consistent encounter that leaves you changed in an irreversible way.

CHAPTER ONE
DEFINITIONS AND DIVINITY

divine *(adjective)*: *of* or *from* God
encounter *(verb)*: to *come upon* or *meet with*, especially *unexpectedly*

The definition above spells out clearly how many encounters with God happen: *unexpectedly*. While you can seek after and fight diligently for these encounters and run-ins with Him, when He comes, typically, you can never figure it out when and how it will take place.

In Acts 2, it says they knew Jesus told the disciples to wait until they were endued with power from on high. So the 120 went into the upper room and were consistently locked up in prayer together. *Expectation* was there and they knew what they were going after. They didn't quite know *what* they were getting into with the encounter or *when* it was coming. Encounters with God are like that; they come unexpectedly, and I personally love that. But the 120 obeyed the voice of God and pursued it diligently, and their hunger and pressing in triggered an encounter. You don't always have to know when or how... but we must know the *what* we are going after.

The Scripture says they were all continually in prayer in the upper room, and then suddenly the sound of the mighty rushing wind came, snuck up on them, overturned their world, and everything was flipped upside down from one encounter. At Pentecost, the Holy Spirit first being poured out flipped the world upside down and trickled down into what you and I walk in *even* today.

This is a true definition and example of *divine* and *encounter* coming together. My definition is a *supernatural experience.* Everything in the Kingdom manifests itself through faith, belief, hunger, and expectancy. Let's start off with laying the groundwork and build a faith and expectancy while also crushing the religious spirit that tries to hinder what we're going for.

What is a divine encounter experience? I would define it as such: *a supernatural experience that invades your natural world for God's ultimate purposes and plan; a divine run-in with God that literally alters your entire destiny and life call.* This definition is intentionally broad because God is so broad and multifaceted in His approach to mankind. His approach to move to, in, and through mankind is broad.

That's why the word divine is "of" or "from" God. It doesn't always have to be *God Himself.* It starts getting complex from the other side, but it's basically a supernatural *break-in* into the natural that has so many different reasons for God's purposes. It's all throughout Scripture from the Old Testament to the New. All over the earth you can see the hunger that we're having in this day and hour—we've got to walk in experience with God like never before.

I'm grateful for all we've tapped into and all we are walking up to this day, but there's much more to be experienced. I'd encourage you to always be in that same stance and posture, a standpoint of gratefulness. The Bible talks of entering into His courts with thanksgiving and praise, and always contending, because there is a fullness out there that we're ever chasing.

This stirs me up. I am constantly contending for a fresh, new run-in with God like never before. I don't care where you are in life. I don't care if you just got born again yesterday or you've been in this thing for ten years, or you're in the marketplace ministry, it's all a level playing field. We've all got to experience Him for greater endowment, commissioning, revelation, and transition. These encounters have so much impacted, that once they hit you, everything changes.

THE VALUE OF ENCOUNTERS

Why are divine encounters so important? Simply put: it's the way God set this whole thing up; He is an experience-able God. You've got to catch this: God is a God of relationship, He's a God of encounter, and He's a God of *experience*. If it's not about relationship, encounter, and experience—it isn't the God of the Bible.

You see, religion typically will tell you otherwise. I had this fed to me as well, and I still hear it to this day. Many leaders and pastors have bashed us. We still love them and bless them. We have these schools for the Bride where those who are so hungry come from all over the nations.

We hear everywhere we go; that people can sense and

feel that there is more than Sunday morning church services. There's nothing wrong with church gatherings; I'm in them all the time preaching. However, there is more! There's a deep hunger raising up in the heavens right now. That's what we really want to go for in the land and help us all to rise up in this hour like never before.

So, to get back to the question, why is divine encounter so important? Because beginning in the book of Genesis all the way through Revelation, we can see this is literally the way God has structured His connection to humanity; through experience, encounter, and relationship. It's His nature.

Another reason why we must live in and out of *divine encounter* is because you can only impart what has been personally imparted to you. This is big; knowledge and second-hand preaching of sermons and things we've heard can only get us so far. But divine encounter actually imparts and empowers a substance in which you can then release to others. This is very, very paramount. I actually learned this by accident.

I got born again at the age of twenty (I'm thirty-nine at the time of writing this). I was really zealous for the Lord and fasting/praying on this journey. I knew very little but I knew I had met Jesus and I was in love with Him. Very soon after that I went off to Bible college. I experienced profound power, not so much prophetic—a little bit of that—but this was the Brownsville Revival, a true outpouring of the Holy Spirit. Wonders and signs everywhere. It was crazy. I spent two years raised up in this. But again, I don't care who you're under, who you run with, or who you know. If you personally don't have a run-in with God, it's okay. You're born again, destiny can still happen, but I'm just trying to stir hunger and encourage you to encounter God one-on-one. You don't have to be in the five-fold ministry or anything like that. But I saw some amazing things during this time of my life in Bible college. I saw the power of God as we'd pray for people and they'd get healed. We saw fruit.

But I graduated Bible school and there was that stirring that I'm feeling again even now as I write this book, that *there's more*. I'm just hungry. I don't know if I know what it is, but I'm hungry in a very good way. But at that time in my life, I felt this hunger come on me and it just would not get off me. I would wake up in the morning and go to bed at night and just knew I *needed* Jesus. So I started searching through Scripture, and thank God for some men of God I was learning from, but these things just started being highlighted to me in God's Word, things I'll touch on later in this book.

I began to see this common thread through Scripture of these men and women who would encounter God and everything would change. Moses was shepherding his father-in-law's sheep, which was pretty mundane, and then *boom*, he ran into a burning bush, then delivered all of Israel. Joshua was under Moses for some time, and knew the presence of God, then they crossed over the Jordan River and the angel of the Lord of hosts took out Jericho. Then there's Gideon, a coward (see Judges 6), and an angel comes to him and makes him a mighty man of God and a hero to Israel.

I saw this common thread with these run-ins and many other run-ins, these divine encounters men and women had that changed everything. When I saw this, I thought, *Oh, that's it!* because up until this point, I had experienced enough of God and was madly in love with Him. I began to see this common thread in all these encounters, and I couldn't help but realize it's how God set it up.

This isn't to make you feel condemned if you haven't had an encounter with God, but to make you hunger for one. Even before regularly encountering God, I would watch this common thread I saw in the Scriptures and see how destiny and life would shift all around these encounters.

So I began to cry out to God because I knew I had to encounter Him. I saw it was the biblical pattern to have a hunger for a one-on-one run-in with God, I don't care who you are, who you've trailed, who you've been an assistant to, none of that matters. It's a divine run-in with God. What do you do when you've had an encounter with God? Have another one. It's just an opening up of His nature and His Kingdom more and more that empowers you, gives you greater authority, and allows you to transform more into His likeness and start soaring through life. I began to see that He's a very experiential God, and it set me off on a journey where I locked a hold of the horns of the altar and I wasn't coming off of it, period. When I found out that "*this* is *that*," this was not optional for me.

Let me encourage you, God's very sovereign and very loving, but He also rewards diligence. Hebrews says He's a rewarder of those who diligently seek Him, and His eyes run to and fro the earth looking for hearts that are fully after Him (see Hebrews 11:6). Hunger is one thing that God cannot overlook, I can tell you. Faith, expectancy, and hunger catch the attention of God. The Bible really says that if you ask in faith, you can just about have anything you ask. Of course, the request has to be in line with the Word of God. But God can't pass up hunger.

To reinforce how you can only impart what has been imparted to you, let me share this. I once had an experience, and personally, I didn't know what I was getting into, but it left a substance on me in this particular encounter. Before I knew it, everybody I'd get around started having dreams and visions. I'd go into meetings and talk about whatever, and all of a sudden I'd pray, and the common theme was these people were having dreams and visions.

That which you tap into in *secret*, will manifest in *public*. Anything you personally contend for and break open in the secret place in intimacy will by default start overlapping in public. You can't work this up, and don't have to even if you could. You'll see the difference in people that haven't experienced a whole lot in the secret place, and that's okay too. We're all at different places, but I'm simply trying to stir up a hunger in you if that applies to you. Often those encounters will be very uniquely designed for your calling, which is beautiful of God. You can't pick what kind of encounter you want—it's got to be handpicked and carved out for your call and destiny.

At this time early on, I started noticing things. The stuff that I would run into by encounter would come upon and had been imparted to me. Then, whenever I was around other people it was just effortlessly imparted to them, no matter what their call was. It's really incredible.

A great example is the difference you'll see with ministers. Often you'll see some who may teach on the same topic, but one of them is teaching from experience and encounter versus another who's teaching from principles. Both are needed, but you start to see the difference is usually between ministers that minister out of encounter and experience, and that there's a substance there and an impartation that can be released from that substance. Whereas teaching from a sheer theological or intellectual standpoint when you've not had a run-in encounter, unless it's a sovereign move of God, you typically won't see an impartation of the very thing being taught on. That's the major difference. The net result of personal encounter is a manifestation of public encounter.

Say for example you hear different ministers that teach on angels and the angelic realm who've had encounters, experiences, manifestations, and the angelic involvement will start breaking out and increasing in other people's lives through their ministry. Whereas others may be just teaching from a scriptural standpoint but without much experience on it. I'm not trying to say anybody's right or wrong here, but experience is very important to encounter an impartation. That's why you see Elisha wouldn't allow Elijah out of his sight till he passed the mantle. It came straight from him. Of course, Elisha shadowed him during his entire apprenticeship, but even up until the end, he wanted Elijah's mantle.

There are certain things you carry and can impart in the same way that they were *imparted* to you.

KNOWLEDGE WITHOUT EXPERIENCE

Knowledge *sans* experience is often much less fruitful than knowledge *with* experience. This is why I encourage you to encounter the Word of God; when stuff in the Scriptures stirs you up, camp out on it and ask God for it. Tell Him, *I want that for me in this area*, or *Make it real to me, Lord.* Whether it be by revelatory encounter, divine run-in with God, ask Him to make it real in an experiential way.

First Corinthians 8:1 says, "Knowledge puffs up but love builds up." I know the Bible also says, "Study to show thyself approved" (see 2 Tim 2:15), but it also says in 2 Cor 3:6, "The letter alone kills, but the Spirit brings life." We see knowledge of the letter versus the Spirit, which is the experience side of the letter. So knowledge alone kills. We need the letter plus the Spirit (experience). *That* is what brings life. It's the difference from the orthodox Jews—they have the same Old Testament we do, but it's complete death since they don't have Christ or the Holy Spirit living in them. It's the letter alone, and it kills. There's no experience there.

We don't minimize knowledge; we have to have it as well. The Bible says study to show ourselves approved, but the experiential aspect of it is all that I'm getting at. Knowledge puffs up, but love builds up. What is love? It's experiential. We need the knowledge, but accompanied with the experience of love in order to really be fruitful. Our pursuit of knowledge has to be accompanied by a pursuit of experience, otherwise—we are missing the points of knowledge and revelation to begin with.

CHAPTER TWO
APOLOGETICS AND ANSWERS

We've laid out a Word foundation in the previous chapter about divine encounters. Whether it's the upper room in Acts 2 or the impartation of grace with Elijah and Elisha, you can't escape encounters when reading the Scriptures. Yet despite these things, you may hear the religious counter it. You personally may be far past this, but others reading this may not be, as we're all in different places. As a result, I think it's important to stop for a moment to annihilate this so you can encounter the *fullness of what God wants* in the following pages.

If you think you're going to know God personally on a deep level and portray Him in the earth in His full glory without experience, I'm sorry, but that's just unbiblical. It's not in the book I read. But religion has this masterful way of putting these lenses over people's eyes that read the same book you and I do, but they walk out this life that's void of these encounters. Again, I'm not trying to be disrespectful. I hope you can read my heart in this. I bless them and I'll meet with anyone on whatever level they'll let me get to, so it's not that I think anybody is greater than anybody else. It's just that we want the fullness of God and what He's really mapped out for us. I'm just trying to call *everybody* higher.

One of the main objections you'll hear from a religious spirit is, "We don't go by feelings and experiences; we just go by the Word of God, brother. We walk by faith, not by sight." Or, "We don't need experiences; that's why He left us the written Word."

I've heard this said many times; you might have as well. The problem with it, is that the written Word of God is full of experience and true faith. They say they're not walking by sight but walking by faith, but true biblical-originated faith *always* leads to experience, encounter, and relationship. It sounds like a nice spiritual-sounding cliché, packaged with quoted verses, but it's actually not biblical at all.

Let's start at the very beginning of the book with the very first encounter, and all the way to the end, and look at some passages in between. The very first encounter of God to man is when He created man, of course, but then God breathed His breath into him. The *ruach* Spirit of God into man's nostrils created life from well-shaped dirt. The very first account God ever had with man was a full-out encounter, supernatural and divine. Then fast-forward a little bit, and God's walking in the cool of the day with Adam. God's very experiential; He loves to manifest Himself and loves to encounter His people. Religion hates that and wants Him out of it. Religion typically has a profound *anointing,* for lack of a better term, for using the *book* to *oust* the very Author of it.

I've seen this happen time and again, and a lot of it is rooted in fear of being deceived. It's based on people who have gone off into a ditch spiritually. Perhaps people have truly gotten off, but that doesn't mean the solution is to then put up such a religious barrier that you don't experience the fullness God intended for us. But the objectors will literally use the Word of God to block out the experience of God Himself, the very Author of it! You've got to be careful not to do that. That which you fear, you automatically become subject to, so anything you fear, you wind up giving dominance over your life to. So if you fear deception, you become deceived. Even though it may be a religious spirit, you still become deceived and limited from the fullness that God intends through experience and encounter, relationship and intimacy.

We need to always fear and revere God alone, trusting in Him and the Holy Spirit to guide us in His full ways, then you stay in the fullness. But the religious spirit just says, "We walk by faith, not by sight," and offers no true encounter.

So the encounter blueprints start with Adam being breathed to life, and ends in the book of Revelation, which was written *from* an encounter. You crack open the Bible, and God's first interaction with man is a full-out encounter experience. You close out the book with Revelation, and that whole book is written based on a divine encounter where John ascends up to heaven, and Jesus is writing letters for John to give to angels of the churches. This is a full-out revelation by *experience!* Not to mention all of the encounters and happenings that are sandwiched between Genesis and Revelation.

TRUE FAITH LEADS TO *AUTHENTIC* EXPERIENCE

I've heard it said, "You don't need experience; be careful brother, even the elect can be deceived; you don't need an encounter, that's why God left us the written Bible." But see, God left us a written Word to allow us to see what all these biblical figures tapped into. The Word is an invitation! It's not merely a record, but happenings that can be duplicated.

Oh my goodness, a burning bush! Are you kidding me? Paul seeing a blinding light. Jesus seeing open heavens! The cloud of witnesses are all on the other side, looking at us—that's why it's in there in the written Bible: to urge you that God is no respecter of persons. He wants to encounter you like the saints of old, yet in a unique way.

There was only one burning bush, so that's another problem with the religious. When they hear you talk of an encounter, they might ask you, "Where is that in the Bible?" Well, where was the precedent for the burning bush when Moses encountered it? It had never happened before, nor since. What about Paul's blinding light? God is so creative and vast, when He encounters mankind, He can almost not even repeat the same encounter. He's too creative, full, and vast. He is full of variety and mystery. So when He encounters mankind in almost every single one of the Scriptures, the only time you see similarities is with predecessors.

With Moses and the burning bush, he was told to take off his shoes. The Lord of Hosts appeared to Joshua, and the same thing was said, "Take off your shoes." Both Moses and Joshua split bodies of water. With Moses it was the Red Sea, and Joshua the Jordan River. Elisha split the water with the mantle just like his mentor Elijah did. You'll see predecessors have similar encounters, but other than that, not many encounters are repeated the same way throughout Scripture.

That's why I want to encourage you when you hear a religious person tell you, "Watch out, don't get deceived!" we've got to realize who we're dealing with here; the God of all the universe who's so vast and who created all the galaxies that we still haven't even figured out. Not to mention the depths of the sea and creatures in it we still haven't discovered and maybe never will ... and we think we can confine Him to, "Where's that in the Bible?"

The end of the gospel of John says that if all the things Jesus did during His earthly ministry were recorded, there wouldn't be enough books in the world to contain it all. He was just one Man ministering and having encounters/experiences for 3.5 years. Imagine what encounters are available to us!

Stir yourself up for experience and encounter. Don't let religion talk loudly and say, "Well, that's just for the super saints." No, it's not at all. It's for everybody, all mankind, and it's meant to be *common*.

Real biblical faith always leads to experience and encounter. It's the substance of things hoped for and not seen (see Hebrews 11:1). Yet it also taps into that which is seen, otherwise it's not even real faith. Abraham is dubbed the father of our faith. If anybody knows it better than everybody else, it would be him. You can check out Hebrews 11, the Hall of Faith, which details all the heavyweights of faith.

All of them had authentic faith that produces literal encounters and manifestations. They were not confined by religion or a fear of becoming imbalanced.

THE FACE OR THE HAND?

God is not uncomfortable with you pressing in for Him to encounter you. That's how He set this up. One of the main lies you'll hear when you encounter religion, when you're talking about encounter and experience is, "Seek God's face and not His hand." But in reality, we're supposed to seek *everything* of God. Jesus told us to seek the Kingdom, for example. Was He wrong because He didn't say seek His face? See, it all points back to Him anyway. He's not nervous about any of this. That inherent hunger you feel, well, He created it in you to want to experience Him. That's why mankind is so hungry for the supernatural—they want to have an experience with God and want to walk with Him in the cool of the day.

Abraham brought Isaac up on the mountain by faith. What did his faith do? Caused experience. They encountered a ram with its horns caught in the thicket. A full-blown supernatural encounter. Then course, an angelic encounter followed. That's where faith led Abraham; to experience. Faith always leads to experience, so people who say, "Well, we don't need to encounter or experience anything. It's not about what we feel. It's about faith."

About six or seven years ago, I was waiting upon the Lord. I still remember the exact chair I was sitting in, and I slipped into a vision where I saw Abraham's hand in the air about to make a sacrifice. I saw that Abraham's hand was shaking, and this really caught me by surprise, as I was just spending time with the Lord and He wanted to highlight and show me some things. Faith is not always attached to emotions. Faith is a decision to obey God, and what the voice of God told you. A lot of times we think faith needs to be attached to the right emotion, but I'm seeing Abraham shaking his hand nervously, and he's probably having doubts. Faith also doesn't mean there's no doubt there, either. It's not the full absence of doubt; it's just submission to faith over doubt by obedience.

Nevertheless, Abraham was willing to go through with it. In Hebrews 11, it says he was already trusting that God would raise Isaac from the dead, who the very promise he received was supposed to come through. But there's a ram caught in a thicket instead. He experienced a full-out provisional encounter by faith, as Hebrews states.

Sarah herself received power to conceive, even when she was past her age (Hebrews 11:11). By faith Enoch walked with God and was taken (Hebrews 11:5). Are you reading this? Experience after experience after experience! Attached to what? Faith.

So for all these religious folks who say, "Well, we just walk by faith and don't need to experience God," that's funny, because 100 percent of the time, biblical faith leads to *experience*. Abraham, by faith: ram in the thicket. Sarah, by faith: pregnant at ninety-nine years old. Enoch by faith: taken by God for crying out loud! By faith, the Red Sea split and the Israelites walked out in freedom on dry land. By faith the walls of Jericho fell once encircled seven times. On and on and on, experiences are caused by faith, not a substitute for faith, as the religious might say. They often use the Bible to set up a religious parameter that's not really biblical and ostracizes God and the movement of the Holy Spirit, which is pretty dangerous.

Imagine Israel walking around five, six, seven days around Jericho. It's still by faith. Imagine the objections: *Yeah right! These big old walls as thick as they are high are going to come tumbling down? Not a chance!* And sure enough, on the seventh day they did because they obeyed. They probably didn't feel it, because to reiterate, faith usually doesn't have emotions at all. Usually doubt seems like it's bigger, but if you're obeying faith, faith's bigger. That which you *obey* becomes *bigger* in your life.

So you have God speaking to you on the one hand, but fear is talking to you on the other, and it feels like fear is louder. In that case, always submit and obey the voice of the Lord, and you'll be okay—even though the other voice seems louder. Doubt can put on a big front by often playing on your mind, your will, and emotions, but as long as your steps are following His voice, it's accredited as righteousness by faith in God and you'll see promises come to fruition.

I felt it necessary in these early chapters to get religion out of the way because the slightest kink in this thing can really hinder experiencing God. You'll be limited if that small, antagonizing voice is still there saying, *Well, this may be for these people, but not me; or, I'm just gonna walk by faith 'cause I don't need experience, bless God!*

So I agree, let's walk by faith, but also walk in the encounter that stems from faith. Faith leads to encounter, experience, and transition. It has *substance.* No amount of religion that you can possibly pile on has the ability to put down a person who's full of faith and set on experiencing the living God Himself.

CHAPTER THREE
PLANS AND PURPOSES

We're going to go into more detail and camp out on a few of these encounters later in the book, but I wanted to share a brief list of biblical encounters that we all might be familiar with. Reason being, if these saints, and even Jesus Himself, had tangible encounters from heaven, don't you think we could use them as well?

- Moses and the burning bush.
- Joshua and the Angel of the Lord of hosts.
- Gideon and the commissioning by angelic encounter.
- Elijah called up in a whirlwind only to drop his mantle to Elisha.
- Isaiah, caught up in a vision, seeing the Lord and the train of His robe filling the temple.
- Ezekiel gets caught up between the heavens and the earth to see visions of God.

- Paul and the blinding light in Acts 9.
- Peter and the Mount of Transfiguration with Jesus.
- Peter has a trance and receives his call to the Jews in Acts 10:10.
- John gets caught up and writes the book of Revelation.
- Philip is supernaturally transported in the book of Acts.
- Jesus sees open heavens.

If anybody *didn't* need divine encounters, it would have been Jesus. I'm sorry, but Jesus' whole earthly life and ministry is full of encounters; walking on water, angels ministering to Him twice, a cloud of witnesses coming to Him on the Mount of Transfiguration (Moses and Elijah instructing Him). Continually in prayer He would see the Father and what He was doing first; prayed all night to pick the disciples. Even Jesus started His ministry with heavens opened up and the Holy Spirit descended upon Him like a dove, and commissioned Him off into the wilderness, which led to Him coming back in the power of the Spirit.

All of these are supernatural encounters, from commissionings to transitions, mantle passing, axe heads floating, Elisha and his assistant's eyes being fully opened, to angelic encounters—this was in a battle season, and they needed this so they had more angels on their side than the number of their enemies.

So for that reason I have a problem when people say,

"Just stick to the Word of God," when the written Scriptures themselves are full of such encounters! Men and women that walked on this earth continually encountering God that helped guide and empower them for God's purposes. The book is full of encounter, all over the New Testament—with the exception of the epistles, you don't see a whole lot of that because they're letters to the churches; these are more instructional. But anywhere where you see minor and major prophets in the Old Testament, the book of Acts, Revelation, the Gospels—it's all experiential. I just want to encourage you to get a new outlook on Scripture, and see that God wants to jump out of this book and encounter us.

Some of you reading this have had encounters, while others haven't. Some, like myself, have had plenty in our lives but are longing for more. There's no end of God with experience and encounters. And the thing about it is the more you encounter God, the more you become like Him. You become more empowered to fulfill His purposes as a result of visitation. The resulting fruit from these encounters is never ending.

God is longing to encounter each and every one of us no matter what our ultimate destiny may be. You may be the housewife, the missionary, a businessman, full-time minister, school principal, teacher, or lawyer. God is no respecter of persons and longs to encounter all. The Bible says that He is the same yesterday, today, and forever (see Hebrews 13:8). If He encountered the saints long ago throughout the Old Testament all the way throughout the New, He's longing to still encounter His people. And much more so this day, I feel, like the last part of the race while preparing the Bride for His Son.

This whole thing is for two purposes: first and foremost, to intimately know God and walk with Him; secondly, to be used by God to touch humanity so they can intimately walk with Him and know Him. It's reciprocal of His Kingdom in a multifaceted way through the five-fold ministry, and through the training of the saints for the work of the ministry. But first and foremost, this whole thing is about loving God intimately and becoming one with Him. Then, spreading His good news so others can do the same. This is even why Jesus is the Bridegroom and the Church is the Bride. The spiritual blueprint of it is in heaven of course, but we even see it in the natural with a husband and wife.

If you have a husband and wife who ride out their marriage covenant solely based on their marriage license/contract and not experience any relational run-ins and encounters, then you've got a serious problem. So if God set this whole thing up in His image, then let's look at it in reverse. Typically we go by heaven's blueprint, and then mimic it on earth in the natural. But for the sake of ease, let's flip that around and look at the earth.

He created man in His image, and you see man and woman become one and the relationship is based upon, of course, some of the letter, the license (contract), and the sheer ethics, legitimacy, and other fundamentals of the relationship. But also one huge facet that you can't do away with: experience of love, encounter, and empowerment one to the other, just like Jesus does to the church.

Imagine seeing a husband and wife who communicate like the religious crowd today. "Hey babe, meet you at the courthouse! Let's ink it up today and sign the marriage license. That way we can make this thing official!" Then they sign the license, and just get in both their cars and go their separate ways. Before departing one says to the other, "Make sure you get your copy because we don't live by experience, we've got the written contract!" We'd think that's ridiculous, because *it would be.*

I get it, we're saved through grace by faith, and that's a strong aspect of this. But again, if you just solely rely on your walk and relationship upon a contract alone, fold it up and throw it in your glove box, how well will you know that person and their heart? Will you become one with them and know them personally, and also produce fruit that's going to change others? It's just how God set this whole thing up. He's very experiential. We don't limit our experience in other earthly contracts. So why do we do so with a heavenly covenant?

Not experiencing Him and trying to have a relationship with Him is like ordering food but not eating it. If you think about everything we do in life—the smells, sounds, the animals, the trees, the wind, the weather pattern—everything God set up (even drinking coffee!) is experiential. So if we take it back to the origin, God's very into experiencing you and encountering you. No matter where you're at in life, no matter how many mistakes you've made in the past, God is very loving and He longs to encounter you.

When Adam fell, God was the first one there with,

"Adam, where are you?" He loved to walk in the cool of the day with Adam. God loves to woo His people by experience. He's the God who manifested His glory in the temple so thick, the priest couldn't stand to minister as there was way too weighty of a shekinah glory in the air. He was a pillar of cloud by day and a fire by night. He loves to manifest His glory and presence. Encounters that happen are revelatory, experiential, and/or angelic.

There are a number of avenues by which encounters take place:

- The Father
- The Son
- The Holy Spirit

The Trinity first and foremost is the means by which we encounter Him. The Godhead can manifest for different reasons and purposes. You see the Father appearing to Christ (Matthew 3:17), Christ appearing to Paul (Acts 9), and the Holy Spirit appearing to the church (Acts 2). There are a handful of other encounters that we see in the Word which came by and through:

- Angelic beings
- The cloud of witnesses

PURPOSES

1) FRESH COMMISSIONING

The biblical way to commission people by God is through encounter. Does it always have to be that way? No, but it's extremely common. The Lord is famous for launching ministries, exploits, missions, trips, transitions, and journeys through encounter.

2) EMPOWERMENT

Without question, encountering God gives you the ability to do what you could not do before. We see this repeatedly throughout Scripture.

Look at Saul in 1 Samuel 10. Saul was just a regular guy until the prophet Samuel came and prophesied the word of the Lord over him and commissioned him as king over Israel. The text says, "He turned," and then the Spirit of God came upon Saul (see 1 Samuel 11:16). That's the divine encounter. The text says Saul became a new man (1 Samuel 10:6). The Scripture says that God gave him a brand-new heart and was totally transformed in an instant because he had a divine encounter where the Spirit of God came upon him. He reigned powerfully until he went off-track later.

It's worth noting again that divine encounters don't happen in the natural. Of course, you can have divine appointments set up by God, but we're not really talking about that. We are talking about divine encounters that step through from the other side into this one, and absolutely flipping your destiny upside down, with empowerment, commissioning, and complete upheaval *in a good way* for the purposes of God.

In the earth, there's plenty of divine setups and happenings, and I love those too. For example, someone walking up and handing you a check for the exact amount you needed to pay your light bill. But that's not what I'm referring to here. So again, a divine encounter is God stepping through that side into this one, bringing the supernatural into the natural and doing so in a way that only He can do in His ways. It's really a beautiful design because it makes us so dependent upon Him. We can't do anything without the Holy Spirit, just like how Jesus told His disciples not to leave Jerusalem until they were endued with power from on high (Luke 24:49). We can't do anything without God. Encounters breed empowerment.

The power to walk out the call comes in the encounter. That's another thing, too, that I love about experiencing God; you can't walk in a certain authority of a calling if you aren't ordained by the Lord, and sent by Him. Good luck fulfilling a divine commission without divine help. It's going to be forced, and it's not going to have authority on it. You may object to my saying that by thinking of the Scripture that says we're to go out into all the world, and we can. But also, Paul, in Acts 16 was wanting to go into certain regions with the Gospel. If we read closely, we see it says the Spirit of Jesus resisted them from going into Phrygia. This is also how keen they knew the voice of God in the triune Godhead, which to me is incredible. They understood that certain regions required a certain grace to labor in.

If you go in what you're not commissioned to and try to operate in something that's not your call, God is gracious and merciful, but you can tell there's just not an ease on it, there's not an authority; it's forced. There's just real biblical precedent for being commissioned in Acts 16. Then Paul has the dream of the Macedonian and they go to Macedonia in authority, fruit, and power.

3) REVELATION

Simply put, revelation gives the understanding we need. It provides the know-how. This is the wisdom to govern the various facets of life that God would have us influence.

4) TRANSITION (REPOSITIONING)

Divine encounters come when you've been going in one direction by God's calling, but then it's time to shift position and transition for a new purpose He has for you. In this case, He'll hit you with another encounter and it will shift everything with a new authority, vision, and focus.

One of the main things I want to point out with experiences with God is there's typically never one final encounter that sums up your whole call. I love this about God; He's so vast and full. There are actually *installments*, and that's why we will have *transitioning* or *repositioning* encounters. I'm just being honest with you; a lot of times I've had this mindset that once your set call is say a certain thing, even in the five-fold ministry, which it doesn't even have to be in, then that's what you are *for life*. That's not really biblical. I'm sure you'll carry that aspect and authority the rest of your life, but you can shift into other areas of ministry. Another thing I want to point out is when I talk about this we're definitely not talking about just the five-fold ministry. I've seen commissionings happen in the marketplace just like in the ministry place.

I remember even in Bible college what was before me all the time was one of the most world-renowned evangelists to date and so by default and by sheer nature, I wanted to be an evangelist. Lo and behold, heaven sideswiped me with this encounter years later that totally took me on another path. I still ended up in what we would call *ministry*, but really, ministry in its purest form is obeying Jesus. It's not somebody behind a pulpit with one of the five-fold titles.

Another thing that's been skewed in church, and I know the intentions behind why it's taught are well-meaning, but everybody says, "God first, family second, ministry third." I know what they mean, so please hear me out in this, but I've heard that for quite a number of years and it's not completely accurate. Again, not to get technical, and please don't go to your church and tell them how off this is. I'm not trying to be a spiritual police.

True ministry, if you want to call it that, in its purest form is the first two commandments; love God first and foremost, and love your neighbor as yourself. And Jesus taught that if you love Him, you'll obey Him. So you can't separate the two. You cannot practically say, *God first, family second, ministry third*. I know what the people who say this mean; they mean it as if ministry is a profession and don't put your family after it. *I get all that.* Jesus said even if you love your father or mother more than Him then you're not worthy of the Kingdom. It doesn't have to be this weird thing, because if you are in pure, true ministry of obeying God, and loving Him, by default you're going to love your family to the fullest and you're going to raise up in the fullness of all He is. So it's not about obeying this perfect systematic priority order. It's about obeying and loving God, and as a result, the rest will fall into place.

The last thing I want to see is for us as a people to box ourselves in with a calling or some arbitrary ministry list. I'm telling you, there are so many unique and ornate niches of the Kingdom God's trying to fill, and so many people are trying to be like Apostle Paul, when they may be a Timothy.

And what happens is we're called to be Timothy but we're trying to step into a Paul, and the authority and grace is not there. As a result we keep running up against walls, there's no favor, and doors get shut. Nobody is any greater than any other. We don't have to try to fit a calling that isn't ours. When it's the will of God for you, it's like a circle peg in a circle hole, it fits perfectly. You'll start to notice this on our calls and destiny that if you get outside of who you truly are as designed by God, you become a square peg in a circle hole that doesn't fit. Far too often I think it's because people are seeing certain cookie-cutter roles that may be more on the forefront before us, and we're trying to force these pegs into the wrong-shaped hole. Just because God encountered you once with a specific call doesn't mean that call can't shift and change. Be open to encountering new plans, graces, and anointings during the soon-coming encounters you'll have with God.

So in closing this section, I just want to reiterate that God wants to encounter us powerfully and frequently. He really does. Often if we will posture ourselves in such hunger and set ourselves apart in wanting to encounter Him, He'll move at a rate that you can't even keep up with. Typically, you'd be surprised at how fast God's willing to move if we're willing to yield and posture ourselves correctly.

The other day I was talking with some friends about how the children of Israel were intended to go into the Promised Land in eleven days. That's to say their journey was supposed to be just an eleven-day journey, but because of decisions and choices and not posturing themselves right, they circled mountains for forty years. God doesn't intend that for any of us, but my point is, I think we often have this mentality that God moves slow or something, but it's usually slowness on our end, not His. He's wanting to encounter us and move in such profound ways at a really rapid pace, no matter what your call is. I've travelled much and I've seen it, trust me. Some of the most profound people running with God and having experiences aren't even behind pulpits, so one can't say these blessed encounters are for the super saints or five-fold ministry preachers. That has nothing to do with it.

Really, when this whole thing is wrapped up, rewards and delegating value in heaven are going to come down to who intimately *became one* with Him and obeyed Him most accurately. That's what it's really going to come down to.

In later chapters we'll get into more personal encounters, and I'll tie them into Scriptures, but this is the groundwork I felt like we needed to establish first. These biblical foundations of faith clear the path and often allow us to dive into the depths of God, deception-free.

*ENTIRE BOOK CAN BE PURCHASED IN **PAPERBACK** AND **EBOOK** FORMATS ON **AMAZON.COM**

Made in the
USA
Middletown, DE